The Penguin Book of
LOVE POETRY

EDITED
WITH AN INTRODUCTION BY
JON STALLWORTHY

READERS UNION
Group of Book Clubs
Newton Abbot 1974

Contents

CONTENTS

6

CONTENTS

CONTENTS

8

CONTENTS

CONTENTS

ABERRATIONS

CONTENTS

CONTENTS

SEPARATIONS

CONTENTS

13

CONTENTS

DESOLATIONS

CONTENTS

CONTENTS

CONTENTS

CONTENTS

Introduction

'WHAT IS LOVE? 'tis not hereafter'; 'love is heaven, and heaven is love'; 'Love is a sickness full of woes'; 'Love is a growing or full constant light'; 'love it is but lust'; 'love is more cruel than lust'; 'Love is not love Which alters when it alteration finds'; 'Love is like linen often chang'd, the sweeter.'

The evidence of the poets is as conflicting as it is voluminous. Even if one sets aside poems about the love of Country, poems about the love of Nature, poems about the love of God, one is left with a mountain of poems about the Beloved, beside which the poems on any other single subject seem but a molehill. And there are almost as many definitions of love as there are poets, because most poets, like most other men and women, have something to say on the subject. In a strikingly high proportion of cases, what they have to say is said better, more freshly, than anything on any other subject. They say it because they have to. Like any other actors in the human comedy, they speak most piercingly when they speak most personally, and because they speak personally their statements are as various as their fingerprints.

Love [Old English *lufu*, Indo-European **leubh*, from the same root as Sanskrit *lubh*, to desire] of the Beloved accounts for many of the most intense moments in most lives; moments generating the emotion that, recollected in tranquillity, may crystallize into poems. Given the high premium that artists set upon intensity, given the relationship between creative and sexual energy, the artist is likely to have more intense moments and more emotion to recollect than most of his fellow men. An artist, moreover, is a maker; one who assembles existing materials to give a substance and a name to something that did not exist before, or something that existed unperceived. The poet assembles words into the likeness of his world, whether it is that seen from his window or seen with his inward eye. He brings them together into conjunctions, into harmonies, that are a paradigm of love; and at moments in the act of making a poem he experiences an intensity of awareness and an exaltation comparable to those experienced in making love. The one may even become a substitute for the other. An ageing poet will literally recall the Beloved of his youth and, in writing of her, bring her to life again.

For these reasons, poets through the ages have written so much, so variously, and so well on this particular theme. But if they cannot themselves agree on a definition of love, no one else is going to be able to agree on any definition of a love poem other than one, like a seine net, large enough to take in all. So I consider a love poem to be not only the lover's 'ballad Made to his mistress' eyebrow', but any poem about any aspect of one human being's desire for another.

Love is a country where anything can happen, and among the multitudes who have crossed its shimmering frontiers since first

> Imperial Adam, naked in the dew,
> Felt his brown flanks and found the rib was gone . . .[1]

there have always been those who made poems of what they found. More than a thousand years before Christ, an Egyptian poet wrote or caused to be written characters on papyrus, which translated read:

> The swallow sings 'Dawn,
>> Whither fadeth the dawn?'
>
> So fades my happy night
> My love in bed beside me.[2]

1. A. D. Hope, 'Imperial Adam'.
2. *Love Poems of Ancient Egypt*, translated by Ezra Pound and Noel Stock.

Before ever man learnt to make graphic symbols of his sounds, he had his love songs as well as his war songs and his reaping songs.

In a celebrated statement about love poetry, one received as gospel by generations of undergraduates, C. S. Lewis declared:

> Everyone has heard of courtly love, and everyone knows that it appears quite suddenly at the end of the eleventh century in Languedoc. The characteristics of the Troubadour poetry have been repeatedly described.[1] With the form, which is lyrical, and the style, which is sophisticated and often 'aureate' or deliberately enigmatic, we need not concern ourselves. The sentiment, of course, is love, but love of a highly specialized sort, whose characteristics may be enumerated as Humility, Courtesy, Adultery, and the Religion of Love.[2]

Since the publication of *The Allegory of Love* in 1936, a number of scholars have questioned, modified, and qualified Lewis's magisterial pronouncements on the phenomenon now known as courtly love. A medieval Spanish and Portuguese tradition of love-songs in which the woman speaks, or in which she is the dominant figure, has been shown to have parallels in ancient Egypt, China, Greece, Scandinavia, Serbia, and Russia.[3] Again, in the most fascinating of all correctives and complements to *The Allegory of Love*, Dr Peter Dronke examines a second archetype of the lyric of courtly love: one presenting what is essentially a man's courtly conception of love. This he traces to ancient Egypt, eighth-century Islam and Mozarabic Spain, twelfth-century Byzantium and Georgia, as well as medieval France and

---

1. See Fauriel, *Histoire de la Poésie provençale*, 1846; E. Gorra, *Origini etc. della Poesia Amorosa di Provenza* (Rendiconti del Istituto Lombardo, etc. II. xliii. 14, xlv. 3), 1910–12; Jeanroy, *La Poésie lyrique des Troubadours*, 1934.

2. *The Allegory of Love*, 1936.

3. See Theodor Frings, *Minnesinger und Troubadours*, Berlin, 1949; *Die Anfänge der europäischen Liebes-Dichtung im 11. und 12. Jahrhundert*, Munich, 1960.

Germany.[1] There is no suggestion of a single torch, kindled
in 'the dark backward and abysm of time', being passed
from one civilization to another. Rather, it is clear that
feelings of passionate love common to all mankind have,
generally by a process of internal combustion, kindled the
poets of different periods and places.

There have, however, been instances of chain reaction,
the most notable in the case of our own literature. It is a
commonplace that the first poets in these islands to leave a
permanent record of their work welded and wielded a lan-
guage 'loud with the clashing of swords'. Like any heroic
society, theirs was a man's world. They celebrated the bond
between father and son, uncle and nephew, liegeman and
lord, the links in the armoured corselet on which the life of
the *werod*, the troop, depended. Their poems reflected that
society, not only in their choice of subject but in the linked
alliteration of their lines. Then, in one of the stranger tidal
movements of history, Anglo-Saxon as a literary language
died on the battlefield of Hastings just as the language of the
conquerors was flowering in Languedoc. The songs of the
provençal troubadours crossed the Channel in the wake of
Duke William's armies; a poetry of soft vowels to be sung
beneath a lady's window, rather than declaimed in a raftered
hall. And slowly, in the way of such 'conquests', the lan-
guage of the conquerors became grafted on to the native
stump, which then put forth a new and vigorous flower.
Three hundred years after Harold's thanes, true to their
oaths, boasts, and traditions, died defending the corpse of the
last of the Saxon kings, an English poet wrote in a language
those warrior forebears would not have understood:

> Your yen two wol slee me sodenly;
> I may the beautee of hem not sustene,
> So woundeth hit thourghout my herte kene.

1. *Medieval Latin and the Rise of the European Love-Lyric*, 2nd edition,
Oxford, 1968.

And but your word wol helen hastily
My hertės woundė, while that hit is grene,
   Your yen two wol slee me sodenly;
   I may the beautee of hem not sustene.[1]

Chaucer's language was new not only in its marriage of vowel and consonant, but in its quieter tone. Though no poet was ever more skilled in the art of rhetoric or had a deeper intuitive understanding of literary decorum, the language came alive under his hand. In some of the first great love poems in the language he reproduced the authentic accents of the spoken word:

Criseyde, whan that she hirė uncle herde,
With dredful[2] herte, and desirous to here
The cause of his comyngė, thus answerde:
'Now, by youre fey,[3] myn uncle,' quod she, 'dere,
What manere wyndės gydeth yow now here?
Tel us youre joly wo and youre penaunčte.
How ferforth[4] be ye put in love's daunce?'

'By God,' quod he, 'I hoppe alwey byhynde!'[5]

For Chaucer, with his inexhaustible delight in the human comedy, love in all its aspects was to be celebrated as the main source of action; and for the poets that followed him, love was the great theme. The Religion of Love produced nobler hymns from Wyatt, Sidney, Spenser, Ralegh, than did the love of God, yet in language the two religions had much in common. The Song of Solomon, as 'mystically' interpreted, provided the love-poets and the spiritual writers with a seemingly impeccable precedent for elaborating either theme in the language of the other. Donne was surely not the first poet to be led to the love of God by way of the love of woman.

1. See p. 64 below, for a modernized version of Part I of Chaucer's 'Merciles Beaute', a triple roundel.
2. *dredful* timid   3. *fey* faith   4. *ferforth* far
5. *Troilus and Criseyde*, Book II, lines 1100–1107.

As the new science of the seventeenth century, the doubts that it engendered, and 'the continuous coarse Sand-laden wind, time' began their erosion of the rock on which the Church was founded, so the Religion of Love was imperceptibly eroded too. Its liturgy, cheapened by loss of belief and by over-use, became increasingly used in a decorative or ironic context. And yet, in the sensual heyday of the Restoration, that tradition retained something of its potency even in the mouth of the bawdiest of the great English love poets, John Wilmot, Earl of Rochester:

> When, wearied with a world of woe,
> To thy safe bosom I retire
> Where love and peace and truth does flow,
> May I contented there expire,
>
> Lest, once more wandering from that heaven,
> I fall on some base heart unblessed,
> Faithless to thee, false, unforgiven,
> And lose my everlasting rest.

It retains that potency still in the work of poets as dissimilar as John Berryman and Robert Graves.

Just as the language of the Church lost its first voltage, so too did the language of the Court. The Elizabethan poets still cast their lovers in the roles of servant, vassal, and thrall, but the old feudal idioms had lost their force. Over the years, *courtship* became no longer courtly and the verb *to enthrall* a shadow of its feudal self. The energizing forces of Elizabethan society were largely materialistic and, naturally enough, they penetrated and then permeated its poetry.

When William Drummond dreams of love, it is of

> The ivory, coral, gold,
> Of breast, of lips, of hair.

Edmund Spenser's lady is

> Fayre when her brest lyke a rich laden barke,
> With pretious merchandize she forth doth lay

24

and Sir Philip Sidney's celebration of the beauty of Lady Rich – 'rich, naming my *Stella's* name' – is itself a metaphor of this newly predominant condition of human awareness.[1]

Good poets more often than not speak the language of their time and reflect something of the changing nature of their society, but a survey of their love poems reveals much that has not changed in three thousand years. The poet in ancient Egypt apostrophized his love:

> The one, beloved, unparalleled,
> more beautiful than all the world –
> look, she is like the Star-goddess
> before a beautiful year,
> of radiant virtue, of lucent skin . . .
> To see her emerge from her dwelling
> is to see her who is yonder, the One.[2]

The first and last word of this song is 'the one', and at its second appearance it refers to 'the sole eye of heaven, the Sun'.[3] The poet, singing the praise of his love, can only describe her in terms of extravagant hyperbole. We are told that she has 'lucent skin', but are offered no more detail on which to feast the inward eye. It is a strange fact that poets who, from the civilization of the Lower Nile to that of the Lower Hudson, have pursued an ideal of precise language, should with so few exceptions have failed to describe the objects of their strongest affections. We look in vain for the features, lineaments of a living woman; for distinguishing marks such as Iachimo reported of Imogen:

> On her left breast
> A mole cinque-spotted, like the crimson drops
> I' the bottom of a cowslip.

1. See Raymond Southall, 'Love Poetry in the Sixteenth Century' *Essays in Criticism*, XXII, 4, for an excellent discussion of this subject.

2. Dronke, op. cit., p. 9.

3. Sir Alan Gardiner, *The Library of A. Chester Beatty*, London, 1931, p. 30.

Why should this be? Can it be reticence in Sappho, Catullus, Donne, Rochester, Byron, Graves? I think not. Love is by tradition blind and, just as the religious mystic is dazzled by 'the darkness visible' of God, so the lover is dazzled by a vision of his goddess, his ideal woman. Moreover, the poet in love and celebrating the fact is often writing for an audience of one; and all too often is only moved to define and describe his love more precisely when he has lost that audience or that vision.

Surveying the great body of love poetry written in English, or translated into English, one looks for patterns, common factors of this kind, but they are few. It is hard to generalize even about love poems written by women as against those written by men. When women write about love, and for centuries they rarely did, they tend to be less afraid to reveal themselves than men; though only Kingsley Amis would dare to say:

> . . . the awful way their poems lay them open
> Just doesn't strike them.
> Women are really much nicer than men:
> No wonder we like them.

Poets are in the nature of things exceptions, resistant to the constraints of bureaucracy, and their poems will not nest in pigeonholes. This admirable independence presents the bureaucratic anthologist with a problem, if he does not want his book to resemble the pavement of Trafalgar Square. I have elected for what seemed to me a minimum of categories, given that I wanted an arrangement more ambitious than an alphabetical or a chronological one. I expressly wanted, in fact, to disrupt chronology and, by setting the poems in a thematic continuum, to demonstrate man's changeless responses to the changeless changing seasons of his heart. A night whisper from the sixteenth century, 'Christ, if my love were in my arms', is as audible and as urgent as any uttered four centuries later.

The anthologist's principal problem – what to leave out –
is particularly acute in a collection of this kind. There are
enough great narrative love poems in the language to make
a book on their own, but because these for the most part are
well-known or readily accessible, and because I don't like
taking scissors to a tapestry, I have confined myself to shorter
poems, sadly setting aside Chaucer's 'Troilus and Criseyde',
Marlowe's 'Hero and Leander' (completed by George
Chapman), Shakespeare's 'Lucrece' and 'Venus and
Adonis', Keats's 'The Eve of St Agnes', 'Don Leon' by
George Colman the younger, 'The True Confession of
George Barker', Allen Tate's translation of '*Pervigilium
Veneris*', and Elaine Feinstein's 'Poem of the End' from the
Russian of Marina Tsvetayeva. In a very few cases, I have
allowed myself to break my rule; scissoring a chapter from
'The Song of Solomon', for instance, on the grounds that it
was a cycle of love poems rather than a single work. This and
other translations I have admitted where they can stand in
their own right as English poems. In the final winnowing,
many such exotics gave place to sturdier home-grown plants,
but I hope a sufficient number remain to show that, just as
the cycle of the heart's seasons has not changed in 3,000
years, its spring can be as brilliant in Dorset as in Persia, its
winter as cold.

I embarked upon this anthology of love poetry to sweeten
an imagination otherwise occupied with the war poems of
Wilfred Owen. My thanks are due to the Warden and
Fellows of All Souls College, under whose hospitable roof
most of my reading was done, and to the unfailingly helpful
staff of the Bodleian Library.

My greatest debts, however, are to my sister Wendy, who
assisted me in my researches and my editing; to Carol
Buckroyd, who helped me plan the book and and to those
other friends who fed me with poems I should otherwise
have overlooked: Mr Nicolas Barker, Professor J. A. W.

Bennett, Miss Catharine Carver, Mr. Sydney Clouts, Professor Richard Ellmann, Dame Helen Gardner, Miss Monica Jones, Sir Geoffrey Keynes, Mrs. Anne Lonsdale, Mr Nikos Stangos, Mr Charles Tomlinson, and Dr J. R. Watson. For the poems that should be here and are not, there is no one to blame but

JON STALLWORTHY

The Mill House, Wolvercote

December 1972

Ezra Pound

COMMISSION

Go, my songs, to the lonely and the unsatisfied,
Go also to the nerve-wracked, go to the enslaved-by-
   convention,
Bear to them my contempt for their oppressors.
Go as a great wave of cool water,
Bear my contempt of oppressors.

Speak against unconscious oppression,
Speak against the tyranny of the unimaginative,
Speak against bonds.
Go to the bourgeoise who is dying of her ennuis,
Go to the women in suburbs.
Go to the hideously wedded,
Go to them whose failure is concealed,
Go to the unluckily mated,
Go to the bought wife,
Go to the woman entailed.

Go to those who have delicate lust,
Go to those whose delicate desires are thwarted,
Go like a blight upon the dullness of the world;
Go with your edge against this,
Strengthen the subtle cords,
Bring confidence upon the algae and the tentacles of the soul.

Go in a friendly manner,
Go with an open speech.
Be eager to find new evils and new good,
Be against all forms of oppression.
Go to those who are thickened with middle age,
To those who have lost their interest.

Go to the adolescent who are smothered in family —
Oh how hideous it is
To see three generations of one house gathered together!
It is like an old tree with shoots,
And with some branches rotted and falling.

Go out and defy opinion,
Go against this vegetable bondage of the blood.
Be against all sorts of mortmain.

INTIMATIONS

Roy Campbell

THE SISTERS

After hot loveless nights, when cold winds stream
Sprinkling the frost and dew, before the light,
Bored with the foolish things that girls must dream
Because their beds are empty of delight,

Two sisters rise and strip. Out from the night
Their horses run to their low-whistled pleas –
Vast phantom shapes with eyeballs rolling white,
That sneeze a fiery steam about their knees:

Through the crisp manes their stealthy prowling hands,
Stronger than curbs, in slow caresses rove,
They gallop down across the milk-white sands
And wade far out into the sleeping cove:

The frost stings sweetly with a burning kiss
As intimate as love, as cold as death:
Their lips, whereon delicious tremors hiss
Fume with the ghostly pollen of their breath.

Far out on the grey silence of the flood
They watch the dawn in smouldering gyres expand
Beyond them: and the day burns through their blood
Like a white candle through a shuttered hand.

Laurie Lee

MILKMAID

The girl's far treble, muted to the heat,
calls like a fainting bird across the fields
to where her flock lies panting for her voice,
their black horns buried deep in marigolds.

They climb awake, like drowsy butterflies,
and press their red flanks through the tall branched grass,
and as they go their wandering tongues embrace
the vacant summer mirrored in their eyes.

Led to the limestone shadows of a barn
they snuff their past embalmèd in the hay,
while her cool hand, cupped to the udder's fount,
distils the brimming harvest of their day.

Look what a cloudy cream the earth gives out,
fat juice of buttercups and meadow-rye;
the girl dreams milk within her body's field
and hears, far off, her muted children cry.

Thomas Randolph

THE MILKMAID'S EPITHALAMIUM

Joy to the bridegroom and the bride
That lie by one another's side!
O fie upon the virgin beds,
No loss is gain but maidenheads.
Love quickly send the time may be
When I shall deal my rosemary!

I long to simper at a feast,
To dance, and kiss, and do the rest.
When I shall wed, and bedded be
O then the qualm comes over me,
And tells the sweetness of a theme
That I ne'er knew but in a dream.

You ladies have the blessed nights,
I pine in hope of such delights.
And silly damsel only can
Milk the cows' teats and think on man:
And sigh and wish to taste and prove
The wholesome sillabub of love.

Make haste, at once twin-brothers bear;
And leave new matter for a star.
Women and ships are never shown
So fair as when their sails be blown.
Then when the midwife hears your moan,
I'll sigh for grief that I have none.

And you, dear knight, whose every kiss
Reaps the full crop of Cupid's bliss,
Now you have found, confess and tell
That single sheets do make up hell.
And then so charitable be
To get a man to pity me.

W. B. Yeats

BROWN PENNY

I whispered, 'I am too young,'
And then, 'I am old enough';
Wherefore I threw a penny
To find out if I might love.
'Go and love, go and love, young man,
If the lady be young and fair.'
Ah, penny, brown penny, brown penny,
I am looped in the loops of her hair.

O love is the crooked thing,
There is nobody wise enough
To find out all that is in it,
For he would be thinking of love
Till the stars had run away
And the shadows eaten the moon.
Ah, penny, brown penny, brown penny,
One cannot begin it too soon.

Sir John Betjeman

MYFANWY

Kind o'er the *kinderbank* leans my Myfanwy,
    White o'er the play-pen the sheen of her dress,
Fresh from the bathroom and soft in the nursery
    Soap-scented fingers I long to caress.

Were you a prefect and head of your dormit'ry?
  Were you a hockey girl, tennis or gym?
Who was your favourite? Who had a crush on you?
  Which were the baths where they taught you to swim?

Smooth down the Avenue glitters the bicycle,
  Black-stockinged legs under navy-blue serge,
Home and Colonial, Star, International,
  Balancing bicycle leant on the verge.

Trace me your wheel-tracks, you fortunate bicycle,
  Out of the shopping and into the dark.
Back down the Avenue, back to the pottingshed,
  Back to the house on the fringe of the park.

Golden the light on the locks of Myfanwy,
  Golden the light on the book on her knee,
Finger-marked pages of Rackham's Hans Andersen.
  Time for the children to come down to tea.

Oh! Fuller's angel-cake, Robertson's marmalade,
  Liberty lampshade, come, shine on us all.
My! what a spread for the friends of Myfanwy
  Some in the alcove and some in the hall.

Then what sardines in the half-lighted passages!
  Locking of fingers in long hide-and-seek.
You will protect me, my silken Myfanwy,
  Ringleader, tom-boy, and chum to the weak.

Patrick MacDonogh

SHE WALKED UNAWARE

Oh, she walked unaware of her own increasing beauty
That was holding men's thoughts from market or plough,
As she passed by intent on her womanly duties
And she passed without leisure to be wayward or proud;
Or if she had pride then it was not in her thinking
But thoughtless in her body like a flower of good breeding.
The first time I saw her spreading coloured linen
Beyond the green willow she gave me gentle greeting
With no more intention than the leaning willow tree.

Though she smiled without intention yet from that day
 forward
Her beauty filled like water the four corners of my being,
And she rested in my heart like a hare in the form
That is shaped to herself. And I that would be singing
Or whistling at all times went silently then,
Till I drew her aside among straight stems of beeches
When the blackbird was sleeping and she promised that never
The fields would be ripe but I'd gather all sweetness,
A red moon of August would rise on our wedding.

October is spreading bright flame along stripped willows,
Low fires of the dogwood burn down to grey water, –
God pity me now and all desolate sinners
Demented with beauty! I have blackened my thought
In drouths of bad longing, and all brightness goes shrouded
Since he came with his rapture of wild words that mirrored
Her beauty and made her ungentle and proud.
Tonight she will spread her brown hair on his pillow,
But I shall be hearing the harsh cries of wild fowl.

Charles Cotton

TWO RURAL SISTERS

Alice is tall and upright as a pine,
White as blanched almonds, or the falling snow,
Sweet as the damask roses when they blow,
And doubtless fruitful as the swelling vine.
Ripe to be cut, and ready to be pressed,
Her full cheeked beauties very well appear,
And a year's fruit she loses every year,
Wanting a man to improve her to the best.

Full fain she would be husbanded, and yet,
Alas! she cannot a fit labourer get
To cultivate her to her own content:
Fain would she be (God wot) about her task,
And yet (forsooth) she is too proud to ask,
And (which is worse) too modest to consent.

Margaret of humbler stature by the head
Is (as it oft falls out with yellow hair)
Than her fair sister, yet so much more fair,
As her pure white is better mixed with red.
This, hotter than the other ten to one,
Longs to be put into her mother's trade,
And loud proclaims she lives too long a maid,
Wishing for one t'untie her virgin zone.

She finds virginity a kind of ware,
That's very very troublesome to bear,
And being gone, she thinks will ne'er be missed:
And yet withal, the girl has so much grace,
To call for help I know she wants the face,
Though asked, I know not how she would resist.

Richard Crashaw

WISHES TO HIS SUPPOSED MISTRESS

Whoe'er she be,
That not impossible she
That shall command my heart and me;

Where'er she lie,
Locked up from mortal eye
In shady leaves of destiny:

Till that ripe birth
Of studied Fate stand forth,
And teach her fair steps to our earth;

Till that divine
Idea take a shrine
Of crystal flesh, through which to shine:

Meet you her, my wishes,
Bespeak her to my blisses,
And be ye called my absent kisses.

I wish her beauty,
That owes not all its duty
To gaudy tire, or glistering shoe-tie.

Something more than
Taffeta or tissue can,
Or rampant feather, or rich fan.

More than the spoil
Of shop, or silkworm's toil,
Or a bought blush, or a set smile.

A face, that's best
By its own beauty dressed.
And can alone commend the rest.

A face, made up
Out of no other shop,
Than what Nature's white hand sets ope.

A cheek, where youth,
And blood, with pen of truth,
Write what the reader sweetly ru'th.

A cheek, where grows
More than a morning rose,
Which to no box his being owes.

Lips, where all day
A lover's kiss may play,
Yet carry nothing thence away.

Looks, that oppress
Their richest tires but dress
And clothe their simplest nakedness.

Eyes, that displace
The neighbour diamond, and outface
That sunshine by their own sweet grace.

Tresses, that wear
Jewels but to declare
How much themselves more precious are.

Whose native ray
Can tame the wanton day
Of gems that in their bright shades play.

Each ruby there,
Or pearl that dare appear,
Be its own blush, be its own tear.

A well-tamed heart,
For whose more noble smart
Love may be long choosing a dart.

Eyes, that bestow
Full quivers on Love's bow,
Yet pay less arrows than they owe.

Smiles, that can warm
The blood, yet teach a charm,
That chastity shall take no harm.

Blushes, that bin
The burnish of no sin,
Nor flames of aught too hot within.

Joys, that confess
Virtue their mistress,
And have no other head to dress.

Fears, fond and flight
As the coy bride's, when night
First does the longing lover right.

Tears, quickly fled,
And vain, as those are shed
For a dying maidenhead.

Days, that need borrow
No part of their good-morrow
From a fore-spent night of sorrow.

Days, that in spite
Of darkness, by the light
Of a clear mind, are day all night.

Nights, sweet as they,
Made short by lovers' play,
Yet long by th' absence of the day.

Life, that dares send
A challenge to his end,
And when it comes, say, 'Welcome, friend'.

Sydneian showers
Of sweet discourse, whose powers
Can crown old Winter's head with flowers.

Soft silken hours,
Open suns; shady bowers,
'Bove all; nothing within that lowers.

Whate'er delight
Can make Day's forehead bright,
Or give down to the wings of Night.

In her whole frame
Have Nature all the name,
Art and ornament the shame.

Her flattery,
Picture and poesy,
Her counsel her own virtue be.

I wish her store
Of worth may leave her poor
Of wishes; and I wish – no more.

Now, if Time knows
That her, whose radiant brows
Weave them a garland of my vows;

Her, whose just bays
My future hopes can raise,
A trophy to her present praise;

Her, that dares be
What these lines wish to see;
I seek no further, it is she.

'Tis she, and here,
Lo! I unclothe and clear
My wishes' cloudy character.

May she enjoy it
Whose merit dare apply it,
But modesty dares still deny it.

Such worth as this is
Shall fix my flying wishes,
And determine them to kisses.

Let her full glory,
My fancies, fly before ye –
Be ye my fictions; but her story.

Austin Clarke

PENAL LAW

Burn Ovid with the rest. Lovers will find
A hedge-school for themselves and learn by heart
All that the clergy banish from the mind,
When hands are joined and head bows in the dark.

Robert Graves

SYMPTOMS OF LOVE

Love is a universal migraine,
A bright stain on the vision
Blotting out reason.

Symptoms of true love
Are leanness, jealousy,
Laggard dawns;

Are omens and nightmares –
Listening for a knock,
Waiting for a sign:

For a touch of her fingers
In a darkened room,
For a searching look.

Take courage, lover!
Can you endure such grief
At any hand but hers?

DECLARATIONS

John Berryman

Go, ill-sped book, and whisper to her or
storm out the message for her only ear
that she is beautiful.
Mention sunsets, be not silent of her eyes
and mouth and other prospects, praise her size,
say her figure is full.

Say her small figure is heavenly & full,
so as stunned Henry yatters like a fool
& maketh little sense.
Say she is soft in speech, stately in walking,
modest at gatherings, and in every thing
declare her excellence.

Forget not, when the rest is wholly done
and all her splendours opened one by one
to add that she likes Henry,
for reasons unknown, and fate has bound them fast
one to another in linkages that last
and that are fair to see.

John Clare

FIRST LOVE

I ne'er was struck before that hour
   With love so sudden and so sweet,
Her face it bloomed like a sweet flower
   And stole my heart away complete.

My face turned pale as deadly pale,
　　My legs refused to walk away,
And when she looked, what could I ail?
　　My life and all seemed turned to clay.

And then my blood rushed to my face
　　And took my eyesight quite away,
The trees and bushes round the place
　　Seemed midnight at noonday.
I could not see a single thing,
　　Words from my eyes did start –
They spoke as chords do from the string,
　　And blood burnt round my heart.

Are flowers the winter's choice?
　　Is love's bed always snow?
She seemed to hear my silent voice,
　　Not love's appeals to know.
I never saw so sweet a face
　　As that I stood before.
My heart has left its dwelling-place
　　And can return no more.

Christina Rossetti

THE FIRST DAY

I wish I could remember the first day,
First hour, first moment of your meeting me;
If bright or dim the season, it might be
Summer or winter for aught I can say.
So unrecorded did it slip away,
So blind was I to see and to foresee,
So dull to mark the budding of my tree
That would not blossom yet for many a May.

If only I could recollect it! Such
A day of days! I let it come and go
As traceless as a thaw of bygone snow.
It seemed to mean so little, meant so much!
If only now I could recall that touch,
First touch of hand in hand! – Did one but know!

Elizabeth Barrett Browning

SONNET XLIII, FROM THE PORTUGUESE

How do I love thee? Let me count the ways.
I love thee to the depth and breadth and height
My soul can reach, when feeling out of sight
For the ends of Being and ideal Grace.
I love thee to the level of every day's
Most quiet need, by sun and candlelight.
I love thee freely, as men strive for Right;
I love thee purely, as they turn from Praise.
I love thee with the passion put to use
In my old griefs, and with my childhood's faith.
I love thee with a love I seemed to lose
With my lost saints, – I love thee with the breath,
Smiles, tears, of all my life! – and, if God choose,
I shall but love thee better after death.

William Barnes

A ZONG

O Jenny, don't sobby! vor I shall be true;
Noo might under heaven shall peärt me vrom you.
My heart will be cwold, Jenny, when I do slight
The zwell o' thy bosom, thy eyes' sparklen light.

51

My kinsvo'k would faïn zee me teäke for my meäte
A maïd that ha' wealth, but a maïd I should heäte;
But I'd sooner leäbour wi' thee vor my bride,
Than live lik' a squier wi' any bezide.

Vor all busy kinsvo'k, my love will be still
A-zet upon thee lik' the vir in the hill;
An' though they mid worry, an' dreaten, an' mock,
My head's in the storm, but my root's in the rock.

Zoo, Jenny, don't sobby! vor I shall be true;
Noo might under heaven shall peärt me vrom you.
My heart will be cwold, Jenny, when I do slight
The zwell o' thy bosom, thy eyes' sparklen light.

Robert Burns

SONG

O whistle, and I'll come to ye, my lad,
O whistle, and I'll come to ye, my lad;
Tho' father, and mother, and a' should gae mad,
    Thy Jeanie will venture wi' ye, my lad.

But warily tent, when ye come to court me,
And come nae unless the back-yett be a-jee;
Syne up the back-style and let naebody see,
    And come as ye were na comin to me —
    And come as ye were na comin to me. —
        O whistle &c.

At kirk, or at market whene'er ye meet me,
Gang by me as tho' that ye car'd nae a flie;
But steal me a blink o' your bonie black e'e,

Yet look as ye were na lookin at me —
Yet look as ye were na lookin at me. —
   O whistle &c.

Ay vow and protest that ye care na for me,
And whyles ye may lightly my beauty a wee;
But court nae anither, tho' jokin ye be,
   For fear that she wyle your fancy frae me —
   For fear that she wyle your fancy frae me. —

Tent take care	*Syne* then	
back-yett back gate	*back-style* stile	*wyle* charm

Henry Carey

SALLY IN OUR ALLEY

Of all the girls that are so smart
   There's none like pretty Sally;
She is the darling of my heart,
   And she lives in our alley.
There is no lady in the land
   Is half so sweet as Sally;
She is the darling of my heart,
   And she lives in our alley.

Her father he makes cabbage-nets,
   And through the streets does cry 'em;
Her mother she sells laces long
   To such as please to buy 'em:
But sure such folks could ne'er beget
   So sweet a girl as Sally!
She is the darling of my heart,
   And she lives in our alley.

When she is by, I leave my work,
 I love her so sincerely;
My master comes like any Turk,
 And bangs me most severely:
But let him bang his bellyful,
 I'll bear it all for Sally;
She is the darling of my heart,
 And she lives in our alley.

Of all the days that's in the week
 I dearly love but one day –
And that's the day that comes betwixt
 A Saturday and Monday;
For then I'm dressed all in my best
 To walk abroad with Sally;
She is the darling of my heart,
 And she lives in our alley.

My master carries me to church,
 And often am I blamèd
Because I leave him in the lurch
 As soon as text is namèd;
I leave the church in sermon-time
 And slink away to Sally;
She is the darling of my heart,
 And she lives in our alley.

When Christmas comes about again,
 O, then I shall have money;
I'll hoard it up, and box it all,
 I'll give it to my honey:
I would it were ten thousand pound,
 I'd give it all to Sally;
She is the darling of my heart,
 And she lives in our alley.

My master and the neighbours all,
   Make game of me and Sally,
And, but for her, I'd better be
   A slave and row a galley;
But when my seven long years are out,
   O, then I'll marry Sally;
O, then we'll wed, and then we'll bed –
   But not in our alley!

Anthony Hecht

GOING THE ROUNDS: A SORT OF
LOVE POEM

Some people cannot endure
Looking down from the parapet atop the Empire State
Or the Statue of Liberty – they go limp, insecure,
The vertiginous height hums to their numbered bones
   Some homily on Fate;
Neither virtue past nor vow to be good atones

To the queasy stomach, the quick,
Involuntary softening of the bowels.
'What goes up must come down,' it hums: the ultimate,
   sick
Joke of Fortuna. The spine, the world vibrates
   With terse, ruthless avowals
From 'The Life of More', 'A Mirror For Magistrates'.

And there are heights of spirit.
And one of these is love. From way up here,
I observe the puny view, without much merit,
Of all my days. High on the house are nailed
   Banners of pride and fear.
And that small wood to the west, the girls I have failed.

It is, on the whole, rather glum:
The cyclone fence, the tar-stained railroad ties,
With, now and again, surprising the viewer, some
Garden of selflessness or effort. And, as I must,
　　I acknowledge on this high rise
The ancient metaphysical distrust.

　　But candor is not enough,
Nor is it enough to say that I don't deserve
Your gentle, dazzling love, or to be in love.
That goddess is remorseless, watching us rise
　　In all our ignorant nerve,
And when we have reached the top, putting us wise.

　　My dear, in spite of this,
And the moralized landscape down there below,
Neither of which might seem the ground for bliss,
Know that I love you, know that you are most dear
　　To one who seeks to know
How, for your sake, to confront his pride and fear.

William Shakespeare

Shall I compare thee to a summer's day?
　　Thou art more lovely and more temperate:
Rough winds do shake the darling buds of May,
　　And summer's lease hath all too short a date:
Sometime too hot the eye of heaven shines,
　　And often is his gold complexion dimmed;
And every fair from fair sometime declines,
　　By chance, or nature's changing course untrimmed;

56

But thy eternal summer shall not fade,
  Nor lose possession of that fair thou owest,
Nor shall death brag thou wanderest in his shade,
  When in eternal lines to time thou growest;
    So long as men can breathe, or eyes can see,
    So long lives this, and this gives life to thee.

Edmund Spenser

One day I wrote her name upon the strand,
  But came the waves and washèd it away:
Again I wrote it with a second hand,
  But came the tide, and made my pains his prey.
'Vain man,' said she, 'thou do'st in vain assay,
  A mortal thing so to immortalize,
For I myself shall like to this decay,
  And eek my name be wipèd out likewise.'
'Not so,' quoth I, 'let baser things devise
  To die in dust, but you shall live by fame:
My verse your virtues rare shall eternize,
  And in the heavens write your glorious name,
    Where, whenas death shall all the world subdue,
    Our love shall live, and later life renew.'

Archibald MacLeish

'NOT MARBLE NOR THE GILDED MONUMENTS'

The praisers of women in their proud and beautiful poems,
Naming the grave and the hair and the eyes,
Boasted those they loved should be forever remembered:
These were lies.

The words sound but the face in the Istrian sun is
　　forgotten.
The poet speaks but to her dead ears no more.
The sleek throat is gone – and the breast that was troubled
　　to listen:
Shadow from door.

Therefore I will not praise your knees nor your fine walk-
　　ing
Telling you men shall remember your name as long
As lips move or breath is spent or the iron of English
Rings from a tongue.

I shall say you were young, and your arms straight, and
　　your mouth scarlet:
I shall say you will die and none will remember you:
Your arms change, and none remember the swish of your
　　garments,
Nor the click of your shoe.

Not with my hand's strength, not with difficult labor
Springing the obstinate words to the bones of your breast
And the stubborn line to your young stride and the breath
　　to your breathing
And the beat to your haste
Shall I prevail on the hearts of unborn men to remember.

(What is a dead girl but a shadowy ghost
Or a dead man's voice but a distant and vain affirmation
Like dream words most)

Therefore I will not speak of the undying glory of women.
I will say you were young and straight and your skin fair

And you stood in the door and the sun was a shadow of
  leaves on your shoulders
And a leaf on your hair –
    I will not speak of the famous beauty of dead women:
    I will say the shape of a leaf lay once on your hair.
    Till the world ends and the eyes are out and the mouths
      broken,
    Look! It is there!

W. B. Yeats

A DRINKING SONG

Wine comes in at the mouth
And love comes in at the eye;
That's all we know for truth
Before we grow old and die.
I lift the glass to my mouth,
I look at you, and I sigh.

Ben Jonson

TO CELIA

Drink to me only with thine eyes,
  And I will pledge with mine;
Or leave a kiss but in the cup
  And I'll not look for wine.
The thirst that from the soul doth rise
  Doth ask a drink divine;
But might I of Jove's nectar sup,
  I would not change for thine.

59

I sent thee late a rosy wreath,
  Not so much honouring thee
As giving it a hope that there
  It could not withered be;
But thou thereon didst only breathe,
  And sent'st it back to me;
Since when it grows, and smells, I swear,
  Not of itself but thee!

Edgar Allan Poe

TO HELEN

Helen, thy beauty is to me
  Like those Nicèan barks of yore
That gently, o'er a perfumed sea,
  The weary way-worn wanderer bore
  To his own native shore.

On desperate seas long wont to roam,
  Thy hyacinth hair, thy classic face,
Thy Naiad airs have brought me home
  To the glory that was Greece,
And the grandeur that was Rome.

Lo, in yon brilliant window-niche
  How statue-like I see thee stand,
  The agate lamp within thy hand,
Ah! Psyche, from the regions which
  Are holy land!

Lord Byron

SHE WALKS IN BEAUTY

She walks in beauty, like the night
   Of cloudless climes and starry skies;
And all that's best of dark and bright
   Meet in her aspect and her eyes:
Thus mellowed to that tender light
   Which heaven to gaudy day denies.

One shade the more, one ray the less,
   Had half impaired the nameless grace
Which waves in every raven tress,
   Or softly lightens o'er her face;
Where thoughts serenely sweet express
   How pure, how dear their dwelling place.

And on that cheek, and o'er that brow,
   So soft, so calm, yet eloquent,
The smiles that win, the tints that glow,
   But tell of days in goodness spent,
A mind at peace with all below,
   A heart whose love is innocent!

Sir Henry Wotton

ELIZABETH OF BOHEMIA

You meaner beauties of the night,
   That poorly satisfy our eyes
More by your number than your light,
   You common people of the skies;
   What are you when the moon shall rise?

You curious chanters of the wood,
   That warble forth Dame Nature's lays,
Thinking your passions understood
   By your weak accents; what's your praise
   When Philomel her voice shall raise?

You violets that first appear,
   By your pure purple mantles known
Like the proud virgins of the year,
   As if the spring were all your own;
   What are you when the rose is blown?

So, when my mistress shall be seen
   In form and beauty of her mind,
By virtue first, then choice, a Queen,
   Tell me, if she were not designed
   Th' eclipse and glory of her kind?

Thomas Campion

CHERRY-RIPE

There is a garden in her face
   Where roses and white lilies blow;
A heavenly paradise is that place,
   Wherein all pleasant fruits do flow:
     There cherries grow which none may buy
     Till 'Cherry-ripe' themselves do cry.

Those cherries fairly do enclose
   Of orient pearls a double row,
Which when her lovely laughter shows,
   They look like rose-buds filled with snow;
     Yet them nor peer nor prince can buy
     Till 'Cherry-ripe' themselves do cry.

Her eyes like angels watch them still;
   Her brows like bended bows do stand,
Threatening with piercing frowns to kill
   All that attempt with eye or hand
     Those sacred cherries to come nigh,
     Till 'Cherry-ripe' themselves do cry.

Sir Charles Sedley

TO CLORIS

Cloris, I cannot say your eyes
Did my unwary heart surprise;
Nor will I swear it was your face,
Your shape, or any nameless grace:
For you are so entirely fair,
To love a part, injustice were;
No drowning man can know which drop
Of water his last breath did stop;
So when the stars in heaven appear,
And join to make the night look clear;
The light we no one's bounty call,
But the obliging gift of all.
He that does lips or hands adore,
Deserves them only, and no more;
But I love all, and every part,
And nothing less can ease my heart.
Cupid, that lover, weakly strikes,
Who can express what 'tis he likes.

William Shakespeare

My mistress' eyes are nothing like the sun;
Coral is far more red than her lips' red:
If snow be white, why then her breasts are dun;
If hairs be wires, black wires grow on her head.
I have seen roses damasked, red and white,
But no such roses see I in her cheeks;
And in some perfumes is there more delight
Than in the breath that from my mistress reeks.
I love to hear her speak; yet well I know
That music hath a far more pleasing sound:
I grant I never saw a goddess go,
My mistress, when she walks, treads on the ground:
    And yet, by heaven, I think my love as rare
    As any she belied with false compare.

Geoffrey Chaucer

from MERCILESS BEAUTY

Your eyen two will slay me suddenly;
I may the beauty of them not sustain,
So woundeth it throughout my hearte keen.

And but your word will healen hastily
My hearte's wounde, while that it is green,
    Your eyen two will slay me suddenly;
    I may the beauty of them not sustain.

64

Upon my truth I say you faithfully
That ye bin of my life and death the queen;
For with my death the truthe shall be seen.
 Your eyen two will slay me suddenly;
 I may the beauty of them not sustain,
 So woundeth it throughout my hearte keen.

Walter Davison

ODE

At her fair hands how have I grace entreated,
With prayers oft repeated,
Yet still my love is thwarted:
Heart, let her go, for she'll not be converted.
  Say, shall she go?
  O! no, no, no, no, no.
She is most fair, though she be marble hearted.

How often have my sighs declared mine anguish,
Wherein I daily languish,
Yet doth she still procure it:
Heart, let her go, for I cannot endure it.
  Say, shall she go?
  O! no, no, no, no, no.
She gave the wound, and she alone must cure it.

The trickling tears, that down my cheeks have flowed,
My love have often showed;
Yet still unkind I prove her:
Heart, let her go, for nought I do can move her.
  Say, shall she go?
  O! no, no, no, no, no.
Though me she hate, I cannot choose but love her.

But shall I still a true affection owe her,
Which prayers, sighs, tears do show her;
And shall she still disdain me?
Heart, let her go, if they no grace can gain me.
      Say, shall she go?
      O! no, no, no, no, no.
She made me hers, and hers she will retain me.

But if the love that hath, and still doth burn me,
No love at length return me,
Out of my thoughts I'll set her:
Heart, let her go, oh heart, I pray thee let her.
      Say, shall she go?
      O! no, no, no, no, no.
Fixed in the heart, how can the heart forget her?

But if I weep and sigh, and often wail me,
Till tears, sighs, prayers fail me,
Shall yet my love persever?
Heart, let her go, if she will right thee never.
      Say, shall she go?
      O! no, no, no, no, no.
Tears, sighs, prayers fail, but true love lasteth ever.

John Keats

I cry your mercy – pity – love! – aye, love!
   Merciful love that tantalizes not,
One-thoughted, never-wandering, guileless love,
   Unmasked, and being seen – without a blot!
O! let me have thee whole, – all – all – be mine!
   That shape, that fairness, that sweet minor zest
Of love, your kiss, – those hands, those eyes divine,
   That warm, white, lucent, million-pleasured breast, –

Yourself – your soul – in pity give me all,
    Withhold no atom's atom or I die,
Or living on perhaps, your wretched thrall,
    Forget, in the mist of idle misery,
Life's purposes, – the palate of my mind
Losing its gust, and my ambition blind!

Edmund Spenser

IAMBICUM TRIMETRUM

Unhappy Verse, the witness of my unhappy state,
    Make thyself fluttering wings of thy fast flying
    Thought, and fly forth unto my Love, wheresoever she
        be:
Whether lying restless in heavy bed, or else
    Sitting so cheerless at the cheerful board, or else
    Playing alone careless on her heavenly virginals.
If in bed, tell her that my eyes can take no rest;
    If at board, tell her that my mouth can eat no meat;
    If at her virginals, tell her I can hear no mirth.
Asked why? say, Waking love suffereth no sleep;
    Say that raging love doth appal the weak stomach;
    Say that lamenting love marreth the musical.
Tell her that her pleasures were wont to lull me asleep;
    Tell her that her beauty was wont to feed mine eyes;
    Tell her that her sweet tongue was wont to make me
        mirth.
Now do I nightly waste, wanting my kindly rest;
    Now do I daily starve, wanting my lively food;
    Now do I always die, wanting thy timely mirth.
And if I waste, who will bewail my heavy chance?
    And if I starve, who will record my cursed end?
    And if I die, who will say, *this was Immerito?*

Thomas Campion

VOBISCUM EST IOPE

When thou must home to shades of underground,
And there arrived, a new admirèd guest,
The beauteous spirits do engirt thee round,
White Iope, blithe Helen, and the rest,
To hear the stories of thy finished love
From that smooth tongue whose music hell can move;

Then wilt thou speak of banqueting delights,
Of masques and revels which sweet youth did make,
Of tourneys and great challenges of knights,
And all these triumphs for thy beauty's sake:
When thou hast told these honours done to thee,
Then tell, O tell, how thou didst murder me!

Alexander Pushkin

I loved you; even now I may confess,
   Some embers of my love their fire retain;
But do not let it cause you more distress,
   I do not want to sadden you again.
Hopeless and tonguetied, yet I loved you dearly
   With pangs the jealous and the timid know;
So tenderly I loved you, so sincerely,
   I pray God grant another love you so.

Translated from the Russian by
Reginald Mainwaring Hewitt

68

Robert Graves

LOVE WITHOUT HOPE

Love without hope, as when the young bird-catcher
Swept off his tall hat to the Squire's own daughter,
So let the imprisoned larks escape and fly
Singing about her head, as she rode by.

Percy Bysshe Shelley

TO —

One word is too often profaned
　　For me to profane it,
One feeling too falsely disdained
　　For thee to disdain it;
One hope is too like despair
　　For prudence to smother,
And pity from thee more dear
　　Than that from another.

I can give not what men call love,
　　But wilt thou accept not
The worship the heart lifts above
　　And the Heavens reject not, —
The desire of the moth for the star,
　　Of the night for the morrow,
The devotion to something afar
　　From the sphere of our sorrow?

William Shakespeare

That time of year thou may'st in me behold
  When yellow leaves, or none, or few, do hang
Upon those boughs which shake against the cold,
  Bare ruined choirs, where late the sweet birds sang.
In me thou see'st the twilight of such day
  As after sunset fadeth in the west;
Which by and by black night doth take away,
  Death's second self, that seals up all in rest.
In me thou see'st the glowing of such fire,
  That on the ashes of his youth doth lie,
As the death-bed whereon it must expire,
    Consumed with that which it was nourished by.
      This thou perceiv'st, which makes thy love more
        strong,
      To love that well which thou must leave ere long.

T. S. Eliot

A DEDICATION TO MY WIFE

To whom I owe the leaping delight
That quickens my senses in our wakingtime
And the rhythm that governs the repose of our sleepingtime,
    The breathing in unison

Of lovers whose bodies smell of each other
Who think the same thoughts without need of speech
And babble the same speech without need of meaning.

No peevish winter wind shall chill
No sullen tropic sun shall wither
The roses in the rose-garden which is ours and ours only

But this dedication is for others to read:
These are private words addressed to you in public.

PERSUASIONS

Robert Herrick

TO THE VIRGINS, TO MAKE MUCH OF TIME

Gather ye rosebuds while ye may,
   Old Time is still a-flying:
And this same flower that smiles today
   Tomorrow will be dying.

The glorious lamp of heaven, the sun,
   The higher he's a-getting,
The sooner will his race be run,
   And nearer he's to setting.

That age is best which is the first,
   When youth and blood are warmer;
But being spent, the worse, and worst
   Times still succeed the former.

Then be not coy, but use your time,
   And while ye may, go marry:
For having lost but once your prime,
   You may for ever tarry.

John Fletcher

LOVE'S EMBLEMS

Now the lusty spring is seen;
   Golden yellow, gaudy blue,
   Daintily invite the view:
Everywhere on every green
Roses blushing as they blow
   And enticing men to pull,

Lilies whiter than the snow,
　　Woodbines of sweet honey full:
　　　　All love's emblems, and all cry,
　　　　'Ladies, if not plucked, we die.'

Yet the lusty spring hath stayed;
　　Blushing red and purest white
　　Daintily to love invite
Every woman, every maid:
Cherries kissing as they grow,
　　And inviting men to taste,
Apples even ripe below,
　　Winding gently to the waist:
　　　　All love's emblems, and all cry,
　　　　'Ladies, if not plucked, we die.'

Sir Richard Fanshawe

OF BEAUTY

Let us use it while we may
Snatch those joys that haste away!
Earth her winter coat may cast,
And renew her beauty past:
But, our winter come, in vain
We solicit spring again;
And when our furrows snow shall cover,
Love may return but never lover.

Pierre de Ronsard

CORINNA IN VENDOME

Darling, each morning a blooded rose
Lures the sunlight in, and shows
Her soft, moist and secret part.
See now, before you go to bed,
Her skirts replaced, her deeper red –
A colour much like yours, dear heart.

Alas, her petals will blow away,
Her beauties in a single day
Vanish like ashes on the wind.
O savage Time! that what we prize
Should flutter down before our eyes –
Who also, late or soon, descend.

Then scatter, darling, your caresses
While you may, and wear green dresses;
Gather roses, gather me –
Tomorrow, aching for your charms,
Death shall take you in his arms
And shatter your virginity.

*Translated from the French by
Robert Mezey*

Edmund Waller

Go, lovely Rose –
  Tell her that wastes her time and me,
  That now she knows,
When I resemble her to thee,
How sweet and fair she seems to be.

77

Tell her that's young,
And shuns to have her graces spied,
That hadst thou sprung
In deserts where no men abide,
Thou must have uncommended died.

Small is the worth
Of beauty from the light retired:
Bid her come forth,
Suffer herself to be desired,
And not blush so to be admired.

Then die – that she
The common fate of all things rare
May read in thee;
How small a part of time they share
That are so wondrous sweet and fair!

William Shakespeare

FESTE'S SONG from TWELFTH NIGHT

O mistress mine, where are you roaming?
O! stay and hear; your true love's coming,
    That can sing both high and low.
Trip no further, pretty sweeting;
Journeys end in lovers meeting,
    Every wise man's son doth know.

What is love? 'Tis not hereafter;
Present mirth hath present laughter;
    What's to come is still unsure.
In delay there lies no plenty;
Then come kiss me, sweet and twenty;
    Youth's a stuff will not endure.

Thomas Hood

RUTH

She stood breast high amid the corn,
Clasped by the golden light of morn,
Like the sweetheart of the sun,
Who many a glowing kiss had won.

On her cheek an autumn flush,
Deeply ripened; – such a blush
In the midst of brown was born,
Like red poppies grown with corn.

Round her eyes her tresses fell,
Which were blackest none could tell,
But long lashes veiled a light,
That had else been all too bright.

And her hat, with shady brim,
Made her tressy forehead dim; –
Thus she stood amid the stooks,
Praising God with sweetest looks: –

Sure, I said, heaven did not mean,
Where I reap thou shouldst but glean,
Lay thy sheaf adown and come,
Share my harvest and my home.

Percy Bysshe Shelley
LOVE'S PHILOSOPHY

The fountains mingle with the river
  And the rivers with the Ocean,
The winds of Heaven mix for ever
  With a sweet emotion;
Nothing in the world is single;
  All things by a law divine
In one spirit meet and mingle.
  Why not I with thine? –

See the mountains kiss high Heaven
  And the waves clasp one another;
No sister-flower would be forgiven
  If it disdained its brother;
And the sunlight clasps the earth
  And the moonbeams kiss the sea:
What is all this sweet work worth
  If thou kiss not me?

Andrew Marvell
TO HIS COY MISTRESS

Had we but world enough, and time,
This coyness, Lady, were no crime.
We would sit down and think which way
To walk and pass our long love's day.
Thou by the Indian Ganges' side
Shouldst rubies find: I by the tide
Of Humber would complain. I would
Love you ten years before the Flood,

And you should, if you please, refuse
Till the conversion of the Jews.
My vegetable love should grow
Vaster than empires, and more slow;
An hundred years should go to praise
Thine eyes and on thy forehead gaze;
Two hundred to adore each breast;
But thirty thousand to the rest;
An age at least to every part,
And the last age should show your heart;
For, Lady, you deserve this state,
Nor would I love at lower rate.

But at my back I always hear
Time's wingèd chariot hurrying near;
And yonder all before us lie
Deserts of vast eternity.
Thy beauty shall no more be found,
Nor, in thy marble vault, shall sound
My echoing song: then worms shall try
That long preserved virginity,
And your quaint honour turn to dust,
And into ashes all my lust:
The grave's a fine and private place,
But none, I think, do there embrace.

Now therefore, while the youthful hue
Sits on thy skin like morning dew,
And while thy willing soul transpires
At every pore with instant fires,
Now let us sport us while we may,
And now, like amorous birds of prey,
Rather at once our time devour
Than languish in his slow-chapt power.
Let us roll all our strength and all
Our sweetness up into one ball,

And tear our pleasures with rough strife
Thorough the iron gates of life:
Thus, though we cannot make our sun
Stand still, yet we will make him run.

slow-chapt slow-jawed, slowly devouring

Thomas Moore

AN ARGUMENT

I've oft been told by learned friars,
 That wishing and the crime are one,
And Heaven punishes desires
 As much as if the deed were done.

If wishing damns us, you and I
 Are damned to all our heart's content;
Come, then, at least we may enjoy
 Some pleasure for our punishment!

John Donne

THE FLEA

Mark but this flea, and mark in this,
How little that which thou deny'st me is;
 Me it sucked first, and now sucks thee,
And in this flea, our two bloods mingled be;
 Confess it, this cannot be said
A sin, or shame, or loss of maidenhead,
 Yet this enjoys before it woo,
And pampered swells with one blood made of two,
And this, alas, is more than we would do.

82

Oh stay, three lives in one flea spare,
Where we almost, nay more than married are:
   This flea is you and I, and this
Our marriage bed, and marriage temple is;
   Though parents grudge, and you, we're met,
And cloistered in these living walls of jet.
     Though use make thee apt to kill me,
Let not to this, self murder added be,
And sacrilege, three sins in killing three.

   Cruel and sudden, hast thou since
Purpled thy nail, in blood of innocence?
   In what could this flea guilty be,
Except in that drop which it sucked from thee?
   Yet thou triumph'st, and say'st that thou
Find'st not thyself, nor me the weaker now;
     'Tis true, then learn how false, fears be;
Just so much honour, when thou yield'st to me,
Will waste, as this flea's death took life from thee.

John Wilmot, Earl of Rochester

WRITTEN IN A LADY'S PRAYER BOOK

   Fling this useless book away,
   And presume no more to pray.
   Heaven is just, and can bestow
Mercy on none but those that mercy show.
With a proud heart maliciously inclined
Not to increase, but to subdue mankind,
In vain you vex the gods with your petition;
Without repentance and sincere contrition,
   You're in a reprobate condition.

Phyllis, to calm the angry powers
And save my soul as well as yours,
Relieve poor mortals from despair,
And justify the gods that made you fair;
And in those bright and charming eyes
Let pity first appear, then love,
That we by easy steps may rise
Through all the joys on earth to those above.

Christopher Marlowe

THE PASSIONATE SHEPHERD
TO HIS LOVE

Come live with me and be my Love,
And we will all the pleasures prove
That hills and valleys, dales and fields,
Or woods or steepy mountain yields.

And we will sit upon the rocks,
And see the shepherds feed their flocks
By shallow rivers, to whose falls
Melodious birds sing madrigals.

And I will make thee beds of roses
And a thousand fragrant posies;
A cap of flowers, and a kirtle
Embroidered all with leaves of myrtle.

A gown made of the finest wool
Which from our pretty lambs we pull;
Fair-lined slippers for the cold,
With buckles of the purest gold.

84

A belt of straw and ivy-buds
With coral clasps and amber studs:
And if these pleasures may thee move,
Come live with me and be my Love.

The shepherd swains shall dance and sing
For thy delight each May morning:
If these delights thy mind may move,
Then live with me and be my Love.

Sir Walter Ralegh

HER REPLY

If all the world and love were young,
And truth in every shepherd's tongue,
These pretty pleasures might me move
To live with thee and be thy Love.

But Time drives flocks from field to fold;
When rivers rage and rocks grow cold;
And Philomel becometh dumb;
The rest complains of cares to come.

The flowers do fade, and wanton fields
To wayward Winter reckoning yields:
A honey tongue, a heart of gall,
Is fancy's spring, but sorrow's fall.

Thy gowns, thy shoes, thy beds of roses,
Thy cap, thy kirtle, and thy posies,
Soon break, soon wither – soon forgotten,
In folly ripe, in reason rotten.

Thy belt of straw and ivy-buds,
Thy coral clasps and amber studs, –
All these in me no means can move
To come to thee and be thy Love.

But could youth last, and love still breed,
Had joys no date, nor age no need,
Then these delights my mind might move
To live with thee and be thy Love.

Cecil Day Lewis

Come, live with me and be my love,
And we will all the pleasures prove
Of peace and plenty, bed and board,
That chance employment may afford.

I'll handle dainties on the docks
And thou shalt read of summer frocks:
At evening by the sour canals
We'll hope to hear some madrigals.

Care on thy maiden brow shall put
A wreath of wrinkles, and thy foot
Be shod with pain: not silken dress
But toil shall tire thy loveliness.

Hunger shall make thy modest zone
And cheat fond death of all but bone –
If these delights thy mind may move,
Then live with me and be my love.

Louis MacNeice

FOR X

When clerks and navvies fondle
  Beside canals their wenches,
In rapture or in coma
  The haunches that they handle,
And the orange moon sits idle
  Above the orchard slanted –
Upon such easy evenings
  We take our loves for granted.

But when, as now, the creaking
  Trees on the hills of London
Like bison charge their neighbours
  In wind that keeps us waking
And in the draught the scalloped
  Lampshade swings a shadow,
We think of love bound over –
  The mortgage on the meadow.

And one lies lonely, haunted
  By limbs he half remembers,
And one, in wedlock, wonders
  Where is the girl he wanted;
And some sit smoking, flicking
  The ash away and feeling
For love gone up like vapour
  Between the floor and ceiling.

But now when winds are curling
  The trees do you come closer,
Close as an eyelid fasten
  My body in darkness, darling;

Switch the light off and let me
Gather you up and gather
The power of trains advancing
Further, advancing further.

John Keats

This living hand, now warm and capable
Of earnest grasping, would, if it were cold
And in the icy silence of the tomb,
So haunt thy days and chill thy dreaming nights
That thou wouldst wish thine own heart dry of blood
So in my veins red life might stream again,
And thou be conscience-calmed — see here it is —
I hold it towards you.

Sir Thomas Wyatt

TO HIS LUTE

My lute, awake! perform the last
Labour that thou and I shall waste,
    And end that I have now begun;
For when this song is said and past,
    My lute, be still, for I have done.

As to be heard where ear is none,
As lead to grave in marble stone,
    My song may pierce her heart as soon:
Should we then sing, or sigh, or moan?
    No, no, my lute! for I have done.

The rocks do not so cruelly
Repulse the waves continually,
   As she my suit and affectiòn;
So that I am past remedy:
   Whereby my lute and I have done.

Proud of the spoil that thou hast got
Of simple hearts thorough Love's shot,
   By whom, unkind, thou hast them won;
Think not he hath his bow forgot,
   Although my lute and I have done.

Vengeance shall fall on thy disdain,
That makest but game on earnest pain:
   Think not alone under the sun
Unquit to cause thy lover's plain,
   Although my lute and I have done.

Perchance thee lie withered and old
The winter nights that are so cold,
   Plaining in vain unto the moon:
Thy wishes then dare not be told:
   Care then who list! for I have done.

And then may chance thee to repent
The time that thou hast lost and spent
   To cause thy lover's sigh and swoon:
Then shalt thou know beauty but lent,
   And wish and want, as I have done.

Now cease, my lute! this is the last
Labour that thou and I shall waste,
   And ended is that we begun:
Now is this song both sung and past —
   My lute, be still, for I have done.

John Heath-Stubbs

BEGGAR'S SERENADE

I'm a peevish old man with a penny-whistle
Blowing under your window this blessed evening
But pause a moment and hear the tune I'm playing

I never was handsome and my limbs aren't straight
But I raise my finger and the girls all follow me
And leave some of the spruce young fellows gaping

I had a painted girl whom none spoke well of
And I had a milkmaid who didn't know cow from bull
And a girl with green flesh out of a lucky hill

And I had a lady as fine and as proud as you
To follow me forty leagues and bed under a bush
And I left her weeping at the long lane's end

And are you sure where you will lie tonight, woman?

John Crowe Ransom

PIAZZA PIECE

— I am a gentleman in a dustcoat trying
To make you hear. Your ears are soft and small
And listen to an old man not at all,
They want the young men's whispering and sighing.
But see the roses on your trellis dying
And hear the spectral singing of the moon;
For I must have my lovely lady soon,
I am a gentleman in a dustcoat trying.

— I am a lady young in beauty waiting
Until my truelove comes, and then we kiss.
But what grey man among the vines is this
Whose words are dry and faint as in a dream?
Back from my trellis, Sir, before I scream!
I am a lady young in beauty waiting.

Christopher Smart

THE AUTHOR APOLOGIZES TO A LADY FOR HIS BEING A LITTLE MAN

Natura nusquam magis, quam in minimis tota est. PLINY

Ολιγον τε φιλον τε. HOMER

Yes, contumelious fair, you scorn
The amorous dwarf that courts you to his arms,
    But ere you leave him quite forlorn,
    And to some youth gigantic yield your charms,
Hear him — oh hear him, if you will not try,
And let your judgement check th' ambition of your eye.

    Say, is it carnage makes the man?
    Is to be monstrous really to be great?
    Say, is it wise or just to scan
    Your lover's worth by quantity or weight?
Ask your mamma and nurse, if it be so;
Nurse and mamma I ween shall jointly answer, no.

    The less the body to the view,
    The soul (like springs in closer durance pent)
    Is all exertion, ever new,
    Unceasing, unextinguished, and unspent;
Still pouring forth executive desire,
As bright, as brisk, and lasting, as the vestal fire.

91

Does thy young bosom pant for fame:
Would'st thou be of posterity the toast?
The poets shall ensure thy name,
Who magnitude of *mind* not *body* boast.
Laurels on bulky bards as rarely grow,
As on the sturdy oak the virtuous mistletoe.

Look in the glass, survey that cheek –
Where Flora has with all her roses blushed;
The shape so tender, – look so meek –
The breasts made to be pressed, not to be crushed –
Then turn to me, – turn with obliging eyes,
Nor longer nature's works, in miniature, despise.

Young Ammon did the world subdue,
Yet had not more external man than I;
Ah! charmer, should I conquer you,
With him in fame, as well as size, I'll vie.
Then, scornful nymph, come forth to yonder grove,
Where I defy, and challenge, all thy utmost love.

William Walsh

LYCE

Go, said old Lyce, senseless lover, go,
And with soft verses court the fair; but know,
With all thy verses thou can'st get no more
Than fools without one verse have had before.
Enraged at this, upon the bawd I flew;
And that which most enraged me was, 'twas true.

John Donne

TO HIS MISTRESS GOING TO BED

Come, Madam, come, all rest my powers defy,
Until I labour, I in labour lie.
The foe oft-times, having the foe in sight,
Is tired with standing, though they never fight.
Off with that girdle, like heaven's zone glistering
But a far fairer world encompassing.
Unpin that spangled breast-plate, which you wear
That th'eyes of busy fools may be stopped there:
Unlace yourself, for that harmonious chime
Tells me from you that now 'tis your bed time.
Off with that happy busk, whom I envy
That still can be, and still can stand so nigh.
Your gown's going off such beauteous state reveals
As when from flowery meads th'hills shadow steals.
Off with your wiry coronet and show
The hairy diadem which on you doth grow.
Off with those shoes: and then safely tread
In this love's hallowed temple, this soft bed.
In such white robes heaven's angels used to be
Received by men; thou Angel bring'st with thee
A heaven like Mahomet's Paradise; and though
Ill spirits walk in white, we easily know
By this these Angels from an evil sprite:
They set out hairs, but these the flesh upright.
    Licence my roving hands, and let them go
Behind, before, above, between, below.
Oh my America, my new found land,
My kingdom, safeliest when with one man manned,
My mine of precious stones, my Empery,
How blessed am I in this discovering thee.

To enter in these bonds is to be free,
Then where my hand is set my seal shall be.
   Full nakedness, all joys are due to thee.
As souls unbodied, bodies unclothed must be
To taste whole joys. Gems which you women use
Are as Atlanta's balls, cast in men's views,
That when a fool's eye lighteth on a gem
His earthly soul may covet theirs not them.
Like pictures, or like books' gay coverings made
For laymen, are all women thus arrayed;
Themselves are mystic books, which only we
Whom their imputed grace will dignify
Must see revealed. Then since I may know,
As liberally as to a midwife show
Thyself; cast all, yea this white linen hence.
Here is no penance, much less innocence.
   To teach thee, I am naked first: Why then
What need'st thou have more covering than a man.

busk corset

CELEBRATIONS

from THE SONG OF SOLOMON

CHAPTER 2

I am the rose of Sharon, and the lily of the valleys.

As the lily among thorns, so is my love among the daughters.

As the apple tree among the trees of the wood, so is my beloved among the sons. I sat down under his shadow with great delight, and his fruit was sweet to my taste.

He brought me to the banqueting house, and his banner over me was love.

Stay me with flagons, comfort me with apples: for I am sick of love.

His left hand is under my head, and his right hand doth embrace me.

I charge you, O ye daughters of Jerusalem, by the roes, and by the hinds of the field, that ye stir not up, nor awake my love, till he please.

The voice of my beloved! behold, he cometh leaping upon the mountains, skipping upon the hills.

My beloved is like a roe or a young hart: behold, he standeth behind our wall, he looketh forth at the windows, showing himself through the lattice.

My beloved spake, and said unto me, Rise up, my love, my fair one, and come away.

For, lo, the winter is past, the rain is over and gone;

The flowers appear on the earth; the time of the singing of birds is come, and the voice of the turtle is heard in our land:

The fig tree putteth forth her green figs, and the vines with the tender grape give a good smell. Arise, my love, my fair one, and come away.

O my dove, that art in the clefts of the rock, in the secret places of the stairs, let me see thy countenance, let me hear thy voice; for sweet is thy voice, and thy countenance is comely.

Take us the foxes, the little foxes, that spoil the vines: for our vines have tender grapes.

My beloved is mine, and I am his: he feedeth among the lilies.

Until the day break, and the shadows flee away, turn, my beloved, and be thou like a roe or a young hart upon the mountains of Bether.

Robert Graves

SICK LOVE

O Love, be fed with apples while you may,
And feel the sun and go in royal array,
A smiling innocent on the heavenly causeway,

Though in what listening horror for the cry
That soars in outer blackness dismally,
The dumb blind beast, the paranoiac fury:

Be warm, enjoy the season, lift your head,
Exquisite in the pulse of tainted blood,
That shivering glory not to be despised.

Take your delight in momentariness,
Walk between dark and dark – a shining space
With the grave's narrowness, though not its peace.

St John of the Cross

Upon a gloomy night,
With all my cares to loving ardours flushed,
(O venture of delight!)
With nobody in sight
I went abroad when all my house was hushed.

In safety, in disguise,
In darkness up the secret stair I crept,
(O happy enterprise)
Concealed from other eyes
When all my house at length in silence slept.

Upon that lucky night
In secrecy, inscrutable to sight,
I went without discerning
And with no other light
Except for that which in my heart was burning.

It lit and led me through
More certain than the light of noonday clear
To where One waited near
Whose presence well I knew,
There where no other presence might appear.

Oh night that was my guide!
Oh darkness dearer than the morning's pride,
Oh night that joined the lover
To the beloved bride
Transfiguring them each into the other.

Within my flowering breast
Which only for himself entire I save
He sank into his rest
And all my gifts I gave
Lulled by the airs with which the cedars wave.

Over the ramparts fanned
While the fresh wind was fluttering his tresses,
With his serenest hand
My neck he wounded, and
Suspended every sense with its caresses.

Lost to myself I stayed
My face upon my lover having laid
From all endeavour ceasing:
And all my cares releasing
Threw them amongst the lilies there to fade.

Translated from the Spanish by
Roy Campbell

Robert Browning

MEETING AT NIGHT

The grey sea and the long black land;
And the yellow half-moon large and low;
And the startled little waves that leap
In fiery ringlets from their sleep,
As I gain the cove with pushing prow,
And quench its speed i' the slushy sand.

Then a mile of warm sea-scented beach;
Three fields to cross till a farm appears;
A tap at the pane, the quick sharp scratch
And blue spurt of a lighted match,
And a voice less loud, through its joys and fears,
Than the two hearts beating each to each!

F. T. Prince

THE QUESTION

And so we too came where the rest have come,
To where each dreamed, each drew, the other home
From all distractions to the other's breast,
Where each had found, each was, the wild bird's nest.
For that we came, and knew that we must know
The thing we knew of but we did not know.

We said then, What if this were now no more
Than a faint shade of what we dreamed before?
If love should here find little joy or none,
And done, it were as if it were not done,
Would we not love still? What if none can know
The thing we know of but we do not know?

For we know nothing but that, long ago,
We learnt to love God whom we cannot know.
I touch your eyelids that one day must close,
Your lips as perishable as a rose:
And say that all must fade, before we know
The thing we know of but we do not know.

Dante Gabriel Rossetti

SUDDEN LIGHT

I have been here before,
    But when or how I cannot tell:
I know the grass beyond the door,
    The sweet keen smell,
The sighing sound, the lights around the shore.

    You have been mine before, –
    How long ago I may not know:
    But just when at that swallow's soar
    Your neck turned so,
Some veil did fall, – I knew it all of yore.

    Has this been thus before?
    And shall not thus time's eddying flight
Still with our lives our love restore
    In death's despite,
And day and night yield one delight once more?

Anon

FOURTH CENTURY

PLUCKING THE RUSHES

A boy and a girl are sent to gather rushes for thatching

Green rushes with red shoots,
Long leaves bending to the wind –
You and I in the same boat
Plucking rushes at the Five Lakes.

102

We started at dawn from the orchid-island:
We rested under elms till noon.
You and I plucking rushes
Had not plucked a handful when night came!

Translated from the Chinese by
Arthur Waley

Sir John Betjeman

A SUBALTERN'S LOVE-SONG

Miss J. Hunter Dunn, Miss J. Hunter Dunn,
Furnish'd and burnish'd by Aldershot sun,
What strenuous singles we played after tea,
We in the tournament – you against me!

Love-thirty, love-forty, oh! weakness of joy,
The speed of a swallow, the grace of a boy,
With carefullest carelessness, gaily you won,
I am weak from your loveliness, Joan Hunter Dunn.

Miss Joan Hunter Dunn, Miss Joan Hunter Dunn,
How mad I am, sad I am, glad that you won.
The warm-handled racket is back in its press,
But my shock-headed victor, she loves me no less.

Her father's euonymus shines as we walk,
And swing past the summer-house, buried in talk,
And cool the verandah that welcomes us in
To the six-o'clock news and a lime-juice and gin.

The scent of the conifers, sound of the bath,
The view from my bedroom of moss-dappled path,
As I struggle with double-end evening tie,
For we dance at the Golf Club, my victor and I.

On the floor of her bedroom lie blazer and shorts
And the cream-coloured walls are be-trophied with sports,
And westering, questioning settles the sun
On your low-leaded window, Miss Joan Hunter Dunn.

The Hillman is waiting, the light's in the hall,
The pictures of Egypt are bright on the wall,
My sweet, I am standing beside the oak stair
And there on the landing's the light on your hair.

By roads 'not adopted', by woodlanded ways,
She drove to the club in the late summer haze,
Into nine-o'clock Camberley, heavy with bells
And mushroomy, pine-woody, evergreen smells.

Miss Joan Hunter Dunn, Miss Joan Hunter Dunn,
I can hear from the car-park the dance has begun.
Oh! full Surrey twilight! important band!
Oh! strongly adorable tennis-girl's hand!

Around us are Rovers and Austins afar,
Above us, the intimate roof of the car,
And here on my right is the girl of my choice,
With the tilt of her nose and the chime of her voice,

And the scent of her wrap, and the words never said,
And the ominous, ominous dancing ahead.
We sat in the car park till twenty to one
And now I'm engaged to Miss Joan Hunter Dunn.

Charles of Orleans

My ghostly father, I me confess,
  First to God and then to you,
  That at a window – wot ye how? –
I stole a kiss of great sweetness,
Which done was out avisedness;
  But it is done not undone now.
My ghostly father, I me confess,
  First to God and then to you.
But I restore it shall doubtless
  Again, if so be that I mow;
  And that to God I make a vow
And else I ask forgiveness.
My ghostly father, I me confess,
  First to God and then to you.

> *ghostly father* spiritual father, priest
> *out avisedness* without thought

Sir Thomas Wyatt

Alas! madam, for stealing of a kiss,
  Have I so much your mind then offended?
Have I then done so grievously amiss,
  That by no means it may be amended?
Then revenge you, and the next way is this:
  Another kiss shall have my life ended.
For to my mouth the first my heart did suck,
The next shall clean out of my breast it pluck.

Coventry Patmore

THE KISS

'I saw you take his kiss!' ''Tis true.'
  'O, modesty!' ' 'Twas strictly kept:
He thought me asleep; at least I knew
  He thought I thought he thought I slept.'

Thomas Moore

DID NOT

'Twas a new feeling – something more
Than we had dared to own before,
  Which then we hid not;
We saw it in each other's eye,
And wished, in every half-breathed sigh,
  To speak, but did not.

She felt my lips' impassioned touch –
'Twas the first time I dared so much,
  And yet she chid not;
But whispered o'er my burning brow,
'Oh, do you doubt I love you now?'
  Sweet soul! I did not.

Warmly I felt her bosom thrill,
I pressed it closer, closer still,
  Though gently bid not;
Till – oh! the world hath seldom heard
Of lovers, who so nearly erred,
  And yet, who did not.

Petronius Arbiter

Doing, a filthy pleasure is, and short;
And done, we straight repent us of the sport:
Let us not then rush blindly on unto it,
Like lustful beasts, that only know to do it:
For lust will languish, and that heat decay.
But thus, thus, keeping endless holiday,
Let us together closely lie and kiss,
There is no labour, nor no shame in this;
This hath pleased, doth please, and long will please; never
Can this decay, but is beginning ever.

*Translated from the Latin by
Ben Jonson*

John Berryman

Keep your eyes open when you kiss: do: when
You kiss. All silly time else, close them to;
Unsleeping, I implore you (dear) pursue
In darkness me, as I do you again
Instantly we part . . only me both then
And when your fingers fall, let there be two
Only, 'in that dream-kingdom': I would have you
Me alone recognize your citizen.

Before who wanted eyes, making love, so?
I do now. However we are driven and hide,
What state we keep all other states condemn,
We see ourselves, we watch the solemn glow
Of empty courts we kiss in . . Open wide!
You do, you do, and I look into them.

Robert Browning

from IN A GONDOLA

The moth's kiss, first!
Kiss me as if you made believe
You were not sure, this eve,
How my face, your flower, had pursed
Its petals up; so, here and there
You brush it, till I grow aware
Who wants me, and wide ope I burst.

The bee's kiss, now!
Kiss me as if you entered gay
My heart at some noonday,
A bud that dares not disallow
The claim, so all is rendered up,
And passively its shattered cup
Over your head to sleep I bow.

Hafiz

The lips of the one I love are my perpetual pleasure:
The Lord be praised, for my heart's desire is attained.

O Fate, cherish my darling close to your breast:
Present now the golden wine-cup, now the rubies of those
    lips.

They talk scandal about us, and say we are drunks —
The silly old men, the elders lost in their error.

But we have done penance on the pious man's behalf,
And ask God's pardon for what the religious do.

O my dear, how can I speak of being apart from you?
The eyes know a hundred tears, and the soul has a hundred
sighs.

I'd not have even an infidel suffer the torment your beauty
has caused
To the cypress which envies your body, and the moon that's
outshone by your face.

Desire for your lips has stolen from Hafiz' thought
His evening lectionary, and reciting the Book at dawn.

Translated from the Persian by
Peter Avery and John Heath-Stubbs

Hugo Williams

SOME KISSES FROM *THE KAMA SUTRA*

The Reflection Kiss, one given
Or blown to the reflection
Or shadow of the lover
In a polished mirror
Or on a lighted wall
Or on the surface of water,
Is called the Reflection Kiss

And is but one of many
Varieties of kiss, for example
The Balanced Kiss is a most
Tender expression, for it is placed
Upon a woman's eyelid
Or on a man's fingertips
And is called the Balanced Kiss,

109

Being neither too strong nor
Too light. Again, the Passion-
Arousing Kiss, that of an amorous
Woman who looks at the face
Of her husband sleeping
And kisses it to show her intention
Or desire is called the Kiss

That Kindles Love or Passion-Arousing
Kiss. And Vatsyayana lays down
Many more varieties of kisses
Besides those mentioned above
(e.g. The Drinking Kiss), stating
That these will not be needed
By those who are properly in love.

Rudaki

Came to me –
       Who?
She.
       When?
In the dawn, afraid.

       What of?
Anger.
       Whose?
Her father's.
       Confide!

I kissed her twice.
       Where?
On her moist mouth.
       Mouth?

No.
        What, then?
Cornelian.
        How was it?
Sweet.

*Translated from the Persian by
Basil Bunting*

Pablo Neruda

Drunk as drunk on turpentine
From your open kisses,
Your wet body wedged
Between my wet body and the strake
Of our boat that is made out of flowers,
Feasted, we guide it – our fingers
Like tallows adorned with yellow metal –
Over the sky's hot rim,
The day's last breath in our sails.

Pinned by the sun between solstice
And equinox, drowsy and tangled together
We drifted for months and woke
With the bitter taste of land on our lips,
Eyelids all sticky, and we longed for lime
And the sound of a rope
Lowering a bucket down its well. Then,
We came by night to the Fortunate Isles,
And lay like fish
Under the net of our kisses.

*Translated from the Spanish by
Christopher Logue*

Alfred Lord Tennyson

from THE PRINCESS

Now sleeps the crimson petal, now the white;
Nor waves the cypress in the palace walk;
Nor winks the gold fin in the porphyry font:
The fire-fly wakens: waken thou with me.

Now droops the milkwhite peacock like a ghost,
And like a ghost she glimmers on to me.

Now lies the Earth all Danaë to the stars,
And all thy heart lies open unto me.

Now slides the silent meteor on, and leaves
A shining furrow, as thy thoughts in me.

Now folds the lily all her sweetness up,
And slips into the bosom of the lake:
So fold thyself, my dearest, thou, and slip
Into my bosom and be lost in me.

D. H. Lawrence

NEW YEAR'S EVE

There are only two things now,
The great black night scooped out
And this fireglow.

This fireglow, the core,
And we the two ripe pips
That are held in store.

Listen, the darkness rings
As it circulates round our fire.
Take off your things.

Your shoulders, your bruised throat!
Your breasts, your nakedness!
This fiery coat!

As the darkness flickers and dips,
As the firelight falls and leaps
From your feet to your lips!

Theodore Roethke

SHE

I think the dead are tender. Shall we kiss? —
My lady laughs, delighting in what is.
If she but sighs, a bird puts out its tongue.
She makes space lonely with a lovely song.
She lilts a low soft language, and I hear
Down long sea-chambers of the inner ear.

We sing together; we sing mouth to mouth.
The garden is a river flowing south.
She cries out loud the soul's own secret joy;
She dances, and the ground bears her away.
She knows the speech of light, and makes it plain
A lively thing can come to life again.

I feel her presence in the common day,
In that slow dark that widens every eye.
She moves as water moves, and comes to me,
Stayed by what was, and pulled by what would be.

Ovid

ELEGY 5

In summer's heat and mid-time of the day
To rest my limbs upon a bed I lay,
One window shut, the other open stood,
Which gave such light, as twinkles in a wood,
Like twilight glimpse at setting of the sun,
Or night being past, and yet not day begun.
Such light to shamefast maidens must be shown,
Where they must sport, and seem to be unknown.
Then came Corinna in a long loose gown,
Her white neck hid with tresses hanging down:
Resembling fair Semiramis going to bed
Or Layis of a thousand wooers sped.
I snatched her gown, being thin, the harm was small,
Yet strived she to be covered there withal.
And striving thus as one that would be cast,
Betrayed herself, and yielded at the last.
Stark naked as she stood before mine eye,
Not one wen in her body could I spy.
What arms and shoulders did I touch and see,
How apt her breasts were to be pressed by me.
How smooth a belly under her waist saw I?
How large a leg, and what a lusty thigh?
To leave the rest, all liked me passing well,
I clinged her naked body, down she fell,
Judge you the rest, being tired she bade me kiss,
Jove send me more such afternoons as this.

cast chaste

Translated from the Latin by
Christopher Marlowe

114

Algernon Charles Swinburne

IN THE ORCHARD

Leave go my hands, let me catch breath and see;
Let the dew-fall drench either side of me;
   Clear apple-leaves are soft upon that moon
Seen sidelong like a blossom in the tree;
   And God, ah God, that day should be so soon.

The grass is thick and cool, it lets us lie.
Kissed upon either cheek and either eye,
   I turn to thee as some green afternoon
Turns toward sunset, and is loth to die;
   Ah God, ah God, that day should be so soon.

Lie closer, lean your face upon my side,
Feel where the dew fell that has hardly dried,
   Hear how the blood beats that went nigh to swoon;
The pleasure lives there when the sense has died,
   Ah God, ah God, that day should be so soon.

O my fair lord, I charge you leave me this:
Is it not sweeter than a foolish kiss?
   Nay take it then, my flower, my first in June,
My rose, so like a tender mouth it is:
   Ah God, ah God, that day should be so soon.

Love, till dawn sunder night from day with fire
Dividing my delight and my desire,
   The crescent life and love the plenilune,
Love me though dusk begin and dark retire;
   Ah God, ah God, that day should be so soon.

Ah, my heart fails, my blood draws back; I know,
When life runs over, life is near to go;
 And with the slain of love love's ways are strewn,
And with their blood, if love will have it so;
 Ah God, ah God, that day should be so soon.

Ah, do thy will now; slay me if thou wilt;
There is no building now the walls are built,
 No quarrying now the corner-stone is hewn,
No drinking now the vine's whole blood is spilt;
 Ah God, ah God, that day should be so soon.

Nay, slay me now; nay, for I will be slain;
Pluck thy red pleasure from the teeth of pain,
 Break down thy vine ere yet grape-gatherers prune,
Slay me ere day can slay desire again;
 Ah God, ah God, that day should be so soon.

Yea, with thy sweet lips, with thy sweet sword; yea
Take life and all, for I will die, I say;
 Love, I gave love, is life a better boon?
For sweet night's sake I will not live till day;
 Ah God, ah God, that day should be so soon.

Nay, I will sleep then only; nay, but go.
Ah sweet, too sweet to me, my sweet, I know
 Love, sleep, and death go to the sweet same tune;
Hold my hair fast, and kiss me through it soon.
 Ah God, ah God, that day should be so soon.

John Berryman

Our Sunday morning when dawn-priests were applying
Wafer and wine to the human wound, we laid
Ourselves to cure ourselves down: I'm afraid
Our vestments wanted, but Francis' friends were crying
In the nave of pines, sun-satisfied, and flying
Subtle as angels about the barricade
Boughs made over us, deep in a bed half made
Needle-soft, half the sea of our simultaneous dying.

'Death is the mother of beauty.' Awry no leaf
Shivering with delight, we die to be well . .
Careless with sleepy love, so long unloving.
What if our convalescence must be brief
As we are, the matin meet the passing bell? . .
About our pines our sister, wind, is moving.

Robert Graves

DOWN, WANTON, DOWN!

Down, wanton, down! Have you no shame
That at the whisper of Love's name,
Or Beauty's, presto! up you raise
Your angry head and stand at gaze?

Poor bombard-captain, sworn to reach
The ravelin and effect a breach –
Indifferent what you storm or why,
So be that in the breach you die!

Love may be blind, but Love at least
Knows what is man and what mere beast;
Or Beauty wayward, but requires
More delicacy from her squires.

Tell me, my witless, whose one boast
Could be your staunchness at the post,
When were you made a man of parts
To think fine and profess the arts?

Will many-gifted Beauty come
Bowing to your bald rule of thumb,
Or Love swear loyalty to your crown?
Be gone, have done! Down, wanton, down!

Anon

EIGHTEENTH CENTURY

I gently touched her hand: she gave
A look that did my soul enslave;
I pressed her rebel lips in vain:
They rose up to be pressed again.
    Thus happy, I no farther meant,
    Than to be pleased and innocent.

On her soft breasts my hand I laid,
And a quick, light impression made;
They with a kindly warmth did glow,
And swelled, and seemed to overflow.
    Yet, trust me, I no farther meant,
    Than to be pleased and innocent.

On her eyes my eyes did stay:
O'er her smooth limbs my hands did stray;
Each sense was ravished with delight,
And my soul stood prepared for flight.
    Blame me not if at last I meant
    More to be pleased than innocent.

E. E. Cummings

MAY I FEEL SAID HE

may i feel said he
(i'll squeal said she
just once said he)
it's fun said she

(may i touch said he
how much said she
a lot said he)
why not said she

(let's go said he
not too far said she
what's too far said he
where you are said she)

may i stay said he
(which way said she
like this said he
if you kiss said she

may i move said he
is it love said she)
if you're willing said he
(but you're killing said she

but it's life said he
but your wife said she
now said he)
ow said she

(tiptop said he
don't stop said she
oh no said he)
go slow said she

(cccome? said he
ummm said she)
you're divine! said he
(you are Mine said she)

Thomas Carew

ON THE MARRIAGE OF T.K. AND C.C.
THE MORNING STORMY

Such should this day be, so the sun should hide
His bashful face, and let the conquering Bride
Without a rival shine, whilst he forbears
To mingle his unequal beams with hers;
Or if sometimes he glance his squinting eye
Between the parting clouds, 'tis but to spy,
Not emulate her glories, so comes dressed
In veils, but as a masquer to the feast.
Thus heaven should lower, such stormy gusts should blow
Not to denounce ungentle Fates, but show
The cheerful Bridegroom to the clouds and wind
Hath all his tears, and all his sighs assigned.
Let tempests struggle in the air, but rest
Eternal calms within thy peaceful breast,

Thrice happy Youth; but ever sacrifice
To that fair hand that dried thy blubbered eyes,
That crowned thy head with roses, and turned all
The plagues of love into a cordial,
When first it joined her virgin snow to thine,
Which when today the Priest shall recombine,
From the mysterious holy touch such charms
Will flow, as shall unlock her wreathèd arms,
And open a free passage to that fruit
Which thou hast toiled for with a long pursuit.
But ere thou feed, that thou may'st better taste
Thy present joys, think on thy torments past.
Think on the mercy freed thee, think upon
Her virtues, graces, beauties, one by one,
So shalt thou relish all, enjoy the whole
Delights of her fair body, and pure soul.
Then boldly to the fight of love proceed,
'Tis mercy not to pity though she bleed,
We'll strew no nuts, but change that ancient form,
For till tomorrow we'll prorogue this storm,
Which shall confound with its loud whistling noise
Her pleasing shrieks, and fan thy panting joys.

Edmund Spenser

EPITHALAMION

Ye learned sisters which have oftentimes
Beene to me ayding, others to adorne:
Whom ye thought worthy of your gracefull rymes,
That even the greatest did not greatly scorne
To heare theyr names sung in your simple layes,
But joyed in theyr prayse.

And when ye list your owne mishaps to mourne,
Which death, or love, or fortunes wreck did rayse,
Your string could soone to sadder tenor turne,
And teach the woods and waters to lament
Your dolefull dreriment.
Now lay those sorrowfull complaints aside,
And having all your heads with girland crownd,
Helpe me mine owne loves prayses to resound,
Ne let the same of any be envide
So Orpheus did for his owne bride,
So I unto my selfe alone will sing,
The woods shall to me answer and my Eccho ring.

Early before the worlds light giving lampe,
His golden beame upon the hils doth spred,
Having disperst the nights unchearefull dampe,
Doe ye awake, and with fresh lusty hed,
Go to the bowre of my beloved love,
My truest turtle dove,
Bid her awake; for Hymen is awake,
And long since ready forth his maske to move,
With his bright Tead that flames with many a flake,
And many a bachelor to waite on him,
In theyr fresh garments trim.
Bid her awake therefore and soone her dight,
For lo the wished day is come at last,
That shall for al the paynes and sorrowes past,
Pay to her usury of long delight:
And whylest she doth her dight,
Doe ye to her of joy and solace sing,
That all the woods may answer and your eccho ring.

Bring with you all the Nymphes that you can heare
Both of the rivers and the forrests greene:
And of the sea that neighbours to her neare,
Al with gay girlands goodly wel beseene.
And let them also with them bring in hand,
Another gay girland
For my fayre love of lillyes and of roses,
Bound truelove wize with a blew silke riband.
And let them make great store of bridale poses,
And let them eeke bring store of other flowers
To deck the bridale bowers.
And let the ground whereas her foot shall tread,
For feare the stones her tender foot should wrong
Be strewed with fragrant flowers all along,
And diapred lyke the discolored mead.
Which done, doe at her chamber dore awayt,
For she will waken strayt,
The whiles doe ye this song unto her sing,
The woods shall to you answer and your Eccho ring.

Ye Nymphes of Mulla which with carefull heed,
The silver scaly trouts doe tend full well,
And greedy pikes which use therein to feed,
(Those trouts and pikes all others doo excell)
And ye likewise which keepe the rushy lake,
Where none doo fishes take,
Bynd up the locks the which hang scatterd light,
And in his waters which your mirror make,
Behold your faces as the christall bright,
That when you come whereas my love doth lie,
No blemish she may spie.
And eke ye lightfoot mayds which keepe the deere,
That on the hoary mountayne use to towre,
And the wylde wolves which seeke them to devoure,

With your steele darts doo chace from comming neer
Be also present heere,
To helpe to decke her and to help to sing,
That all the woods may answer and your eccho ring.

Wake now, my love, awake; for it is time.
The Rosy Morne long since left Tithones bed,
All ready to her silver coche to clyme,
And Phoebus gins to shew his glorious hed.
Hark how the cheerefull birds do chaunt theyr laies
And carroll of loves praise.
The merry Larke hir mattins sings aloft,
The thrush replyes, the Mavis descant playes,
The Ouzell shrills, the Ruddock warbles soft,
So goodly all agree with sweet consent,
To this dayes merriment.
Ah my deere love, why doe ye sleepe thus long,
When meeter were that ye should now awake,
T'awayt the comming of your joyous make,
And hearken to the birds lovelearned song,
The deawy leaves among.
For they of joy and pleasance to you sing,
That all the woods them answer and theyr eccho ring.

My love is now awake out of her dreame,
And her fayre eyes, like stars that dimmed were
With darksome cloud, now shew theyr goodly beams
More bright then Hesperus his head doth rere.
Come now, ye damzels, daughters of delight,
Helpe quickly her to dight,
But first come, ye fayre houres which were begot
In Joves sweet paradice, of Day and Night,
Which doe the seasons of the yeare allot,
And al that ever in this world is fayre
Doe make and still repayre.

And ye three handmayds of the Cyprian Queene,
The which doe still adorne her beauties pride,
Helpe to addorne my beautifullest bride:
And as ye her array, still throw betweene
Some graces to be seene,
And as ye use to Venus, to her sing,
The whiles the woods shal answer and your eccho ring.

Now is my love all ready forth to come;
Let all the virgins therefore well awayt,
And ye fresh boyes that tend upon her groome
Prepare your selves; for he is comming strayt.
Set all your things in seemely good aray
Fit for so joyfull day,
The joyfulst day that ever sunne did see.
Faire Sun, shew forth thy favourable ray,
And let thy lifull heat not fervent be
For feare of burning her sunshyny face,
Her beauty to disgrace.
O fayrest Phoebus, father of the Muse
If ever I did honour thee aright,
Or sing the thing, that mote thy mind delight,
Doe not thy servants simple boone refuse,
But let this day, let this one day, be myne,
Let all the rest be thine.
Then I thy soverayne prayses loud wil sing,
That all the woods shal answer and theyr eccho ring.

Harke how the Minstrels gin to shrill aloud
Their merry Musick that resounds from far,
The pipe, the tabor, and the trembling Croud,
That well agree withouten breach or jar.
But most of all the Damzels doe delite,
When they their tymbrels smyte,
And thereunto doe daunce and carrol sweet,

That all the sences they doe ravish quite,
The whyles the boyes run up and downe the street,
Crying aloud with strong confused noyce,
As if it were one voyce.
Hymen, io, Hymen, Hymen, they do shout,
That even to the heavens theyr shouting shrill
Doth reach, and all the firmament doth fill,
To which the people standing all about,
As in approvance doe thereto applaud
And loud advance her laud,
And evermore they Hymen, Hymen sing,
That al the woods them answer and theyr eccho ring.

Loe where she comes along with portly pace
Lyke Phoebe from her chamber of the East,
Arysing forth to run her mighty race,
Clad all in white, that seemes a virgin best.
So well it her beseemes that ye would weene
Some angell she had beene.
Her long loose yellow locks lyke golden wyre,
Sprinckled with perle, and perling flowres a tweene,
Doe lyke a golden mantle her attyre,
And being crowned with a girland greene,
Seeme lyke some mayden Queene.
Her modest eyes abashed to behold
So many gazers, as on her do stare,
Upon the lowly ground affixed are.
Ne dare lift up her countenance too bold,
But blush to heare her prayses sung so loud,
So farre from being proud.
Nathlesse doe ye still loud her prayses sing.
That all the woods may answer and your eccho ring.
Tell me, ye merchants daughters, did ye see
So fayre a creature in your towne before,
So sweet, so lovely, and so mild as she,

Adornd with beautyes grace and vertues store,
Her goodly eyes lyke Saphyres shining bright,
Her forehead yvory white,
Her cheekes lyke apples which the sun hath rudded,
Her lips lyke cherryes charming men to byte,
Her brest like to a bowle of creame uncrudded,
Her paps lyke lyllies budded,
Her snowie necke lyke to a marble towre,
And all her body like a pallace fayre,
Ascending uppe with many a stately stayre,
To honors seat and chastities sweet bowre.
Why stand ye still, ye virgins, in amaze,
Upon her so to gaze,
Whiles ye forget your former lay to sing,
To which the woods did answer and your eccho ring

But if ye saw that which no eyes can see,
The inward beauty of her lively spright,
Garnisht with heavenly guifts of high degree,
Much more then would ye wonder at that sight,
And stand astonisht lyke to those which red
Medusaes mazeful hed.
There dwels sweet love and constant chastity,
Unspotted fayth and comely womanhood,
Regard of honour and mild modesty,
There vertue raynes as Queene in royal throne,
And giveth lawes alone.
The which the base affections doe obay,
And yeeld theyr services unto her will,
Ne thought of thing uncomely ever may
Thereto approach to tempt her mind to ill.
Had ye once seene these her celestial threasures,
And unrevealed pleasures,
Then would ye wonder and her prayses sing,
That al the woods should answer and your echo ring.

Open the temple gates unto my love,
Open them wide that she may enter in,
And all the postes adorne as doth behove,
And all the pillours deck with girlands trim,
For to recyve this Saynt with honour dew,
That commeth in to you.
With trembling steps and humble reverence,
She commeth in, before th'almighties vew,
Of her, ye virgins, learne obedience,
When so ye come into those holy places,
To humble your proud faces:
Bring her up to th'high altar, that she may
The sacred ceremonies there partake,
The which do endlesse matrimony make,
And let the roring Organs loudly play
The praises of the Lord in lively notes,
The whiles with hollow throates
The Choristers the joyous Antheme sing,
That al the woods may answere and their eccho ring.

Behold whiles she before the altar stands
Hearing the holy priest that to her speakes
And blesseth her with his two happy hands,
How the red roses flush up in her cheekes,
And the pure snow with goodly vermill stayne,
Like crimsin dyde in grayne,
That even th'Angels which continually
About the sacred Altare doe remaine,
Forget their service and about her fly,
Ofte peeping in her face that seemes more fayre,
The more they on it stare.
But her sad eyes still fastened on the ground,
Are governed with goodly modesty,
That suffers not one looke to glaunce awry,
Which may let in a little thought unsownd.

Why blush ye, love, to give to me your hand,
The pledge of all our band?
Sing ye, sweet Angels, Alleluya sing,
That all the woods may answere and your eccho ring.

Now al is done; bring home the bride againe,
Bring home the triumph of our victory,
Bring home with you the glory of her gaine,
With joyance bring her and with jollity.
Never had man more joyfull day then this,
Whom heaven would heape with blis.
Make feast therefore now all this live long day,
This day for ever to me holy is,
Poure out the wine without restraint or stay,
Poure not by cups, but by the belly full,
Poure out to all that wull,
And sprinkle all the postes and wals with wine,
That they may sweat, and drunken be withall.
Crowne ye God Bacchus with a coronall,
And Hymen also crowne with wreathes of vine,
And let the Graces daunce unto the rest;
For they can doo it best:
The whiles the maydens doe theyr carroll sing,
To which the woods shal answer and theyr eccho ring.

Ring ye the bels, ye yong men of the towne,
And leave your wonted labors for this day:
This day is holy; doe ye write it downe,
That ye for ever it remember may.
This day the sunne is in his chiefest hight,
With Barnaby the bright,
From whence declining daily by degrees,
He somewhat loseth of his heat and light,
When once the Crab behind his back he sees.
But for this time it ill ordained was,

To chose the longest day in all the yeare,
And shortest night, when longest fitter weare:
Yet never day so long, but late would passe.
Ring ye the bels, to make it weare away,
And bonefiers make all day,
And daunce about them, and about them sing,
That all the woods may answer, and your eccho ring.

Ah when will this long weary day have end,
And lende me leave to come unto my love?
How slowly do the houres theyr numbers spend!
How slowly does sad Time his feathers move!
Hast thee, O fayrest Planet, to thy home
Within the Westerne fome:
Thy tyred steedes long since have need of rest.
Long though it be, at last I see it gloome,
And the bright evening star with golden creast
Appeare out of the East.
Fayre childe of beauty, glorious lampe of love,
That all the host of heaven in rankes doost lead,
And guydest lovers through the nightes dread,
How chearefully thou lookest from above,
And seemst to laugh atweene thy twinkling light
As joying in the sight
Of these glad many which for joy doe sing,
That all the woods them answer and their echo ring.

Now ceasse, ye damsels, your delights forepast;
Enough is it, that all the day was youres:
Now day is doen, and night is nighing fast:
Now bring the Bryde into the brydall boures.
Now night is come, now soone her disaray,
And in her bed her lay;
Lay her in lillies and in violets,
And silken courteins over her display,

And odourd sheetes, and Arras coverlets.
Behold how goodly my faire love does ly
In proud humility;
Like unto Maia, when as Jove her tooke,
In Tempe, lying on the flowry gras,
Twixt sleepe and wake, after she weary was,
With bathing in the Acidalian brooke.
Now it is night, ye damsels may be gon,
And leave my love alone,
And leave likewise your former lay to sing:
The woods no more shal answere, nor your echo ring.

Now welcome night, thou night so long expected,
That long daies labour doest at last defray,
And all my cares, which cruell love collected,
Hast sumd in one, and cancelled for aye:
Spread thy broad wing over my love and me,
That no man may us see,
And in thy sable mantle us enwrap,
From feare of perrill and foule horror free.
Let no false treason seeke us to entrap,
Nor any dread disquiet once annoy
The safety of our joy:
But let the night be calme and quietsome,
Without tempestuous storms or sad afray:
Lyke as when Jove with fayre Alcmena lay,
When he begot the great Tirynthian groome:
Or lyke as when he with thy selfe did lie,
And begot Majesty.
And let the mayds and yongmen cease to sing:
Ne let the woods them answer, nor theyr eccho ring.

Let no lamenting cryes, nor dolefull teares,
Be heard all night within nor yet without:
Ne let false whispers, breeding hidden feares,

Breake gentle sleepe with misconceived dout.
Let no deluding dreames, nor dreadful sights
Make sudden sad affrights;
Ne let housefyres, nor lightnings helpelesse harmes,
Ne let the Pouke, nor other evill sprights,
Ne let mischivous witches with theyr charmes,
Ne let hob Goblins, names whose sence we see not,
Fray us with things that be not.
Let not the shriech Oule, nor the Storke be heard,
Nor the night Raven that still deadly yels,
Nor damned ghosts cald up with mighty spels,
Nor griesly vultures make us once affeard,
Ne let th'unpleasant Quyre of Frogs still croking
Make us to wish theyr choking.
Let none of these theyr drery accents sing;
Ne let the woods them answer, nor theyr eccho ring.

But let stil Silence trew night watches keepe,
That sacred peace may in assurance rayne,
And tymely sleep, when it is tyme to sleepe,
May poure his limbs forth on your pleasant playne,
The whiles an hundred little winged loves,
Like divers fethered doves,
Shall fly and flutter round about your bed,
And in the secret darke, that none reproves,
Their prety stealthes shal worke, and snares shal spread
To filch away sweet snatches of delight,
Conceald through covert night.
Ye sonnes of Venus, play your sports at will,
For greedy pleasure, carelesse of your toyes,
Thinks more upon her paradise of joyes,
Then what ye do, albe it good or ill.
All night therefore attend your merry play,
For it will soone be day:
Now none doth hinder you, that say or sing,

132

Ne will the woods now answer, nor your Eccho ring.
Who is the same, which at my window peepes?
Or whose is that faire face, that shines so bright,
Is it not Cinthia, she that never sleepes,
But walkes about high heaven al the night?
O fayrest goddesse, do thou not envy
My love with me to spy:
For thou likewise didst love, though now unthought,
And for a fleece of woll, which privily
The Latmian shephard once unto thee brought,
His pleasures with thee wrought.
Therefore to us be favorable now;
And sith of wemens labours thou hast charge,
And generation goodly dost enlarge,
Encline thy will t'effect our wishfull vow,
And the chast wombe informe with timely seed,
That may our comfort breed:
Till which we cease our hopefull hap to sing,
Ne let the woods us answere, nor our Eccho ring.

And thou, great Juno, which with awful might
The lawes of wedlock still dost patronize,
And the religion of the faith first plight
With sacred rites hast taught to solemnize:
And eeke for comfort often called art
Of women in their smart,
Eternally bind thou this lovely band,
And all thy blessings unto us impart.
And thou, glad Genius, in whose gentle hand
The bridale bowre and geniall bed remaine,
Without blemish or staine,
And the sweet pleasures of theyr loves delight
With secret ayde doest succour and supply,
Till they bring forth the fruitfull progeny,
Send us the timely fruit of this same night.

And thou, fayre Hebe, and thou, Hymen free,
Grant that it may so be.
Til which we cease your further prayse to sing,
Ne any woods shal answer, nor your Eccho ring.

And ye high heavens, the temple of the gods,
In which a thousand torches flaming bright
Doe burne, that to us wretched earthly clods
In dreadful darknesse lend desired light;
And all ye powers which in the same remayne,
More than we men can fayne,
Poure out your blessing on us plentiously
And happy influence upon us raine,
That we may raise a large posterity,
Which from the earth, which they may long possesse,
With lasting happinesse,
Up to your haughty pallaces may mount,
And for the guerdon of theyr glorious merit
May heavenly tabernacles there inherit,
Of blessed Saints for to increase the count.
So let us rest, sweet love, in hope of this,
And cease till then our tymely joyes to sing,
The woods no more us answer, nor our eccho ring.

Song, made in lieu of many ornaments,
With which my love should duly have bene dect,
Which cutting off through hasty accidents,
Ye would not stay your dew time to expect,
But promist both to recompens,
Be unto her a goodly ornament,
And for short time an endlesse moniment.

Tead torch	*Croud* fiddle
dight dress	*Livful* life-giving
diapred patterned	*mazeful* amazing
make mate	*sad* serious
weene think	*querdon* reward

134

Walt Whitman

From pent-up, aching rivers;
From that of myself, without which I were nothing;
From what I am determined to make illustrious, even if I
    stand sole among men;
From my own voice resonant – singing the phallus,
Singing the song of procreation,
Singing the need of superb children, and therein superb
    grown people,
Singing the muscular urge and the blending,
Singing the bedfellow's song, (O resistless yearning!
O for any and each, the body correlative attracting!
O for you, whoever you are, your correlative body! O it,
    more than all else, you delighting!)
– From the hungry gnaw that eats me night and day;
From native moments – from bashful pains – singing
    them;
Singing something yet unfound, though I have diligently
    sought it, many a long year,
Singing the true song of the Soul, fitful, at random;
Singing what, to the Soul, entirely redeemed her, the faith-
    ful one, even the prostitute, who detained me when I
    went to the city;
Singing the song of prostitutes;
Renascent with grossest Nature, or among animals;
Of that – of them, and what goes with them, my poems
    informing;
Of the smell of apples and lemons – of the pairing of birds,
Of the wet of woods – of the lapping of waves,
Of the mad pushes of waves upon the land – I them
    chanting;

The overture lightly sounding – the strain anticipating;
The welcome nearness – the sight of the perfect body;
The swimmer swimming naked in the bath, or motionless
   on his back lying and floating;
The female form approaching – I, pensive, love-flesh
   tremulous, aching;
The divine list, for myself or you, or for any one, making;
The face – the limbs – the index from head to foot, and
   what it arouses;
The mystic deliria – the madness amorous – the utter
   abandonment;
(Hark close, and still, what I now whisper to you,
I love you – O you entirely possess me,
O I wish that you and I escape from the rest, and go
   utterly off – O free and lawless,
Two hawks in the air – two fishes swimming in the sea
   not more lawless than we;)
– The furious storm through me careering – I passionately
   trembling;
The oath of the inseparableness of two together – of the
   woman that loves me, and whom I love more than my
   life – that oath swearing;
(O I willingly stake all, for you!
O let me be lost, if it must be so!
O you and I – what is it to us what the rest do or think?
What is all else to us? only that we enjoy each other, and
   exhaust each other, if it must be so:)
– From the master – the pilot I yield the vessel to;
The general commanding me, commanding all – from him
   permission taking;
From time the programme hastening, (I have loitered too
   long, as it is;)
From sex – From the warp and from the woof;
(To talk to the perfect girl who understands me,

To waft to her these from my own lips – to effuse them
　　from my own body;)
From privacy – from frequent repinings alone;
From plenty of persons near, and yet the right person not
　　near;
From the soft sliding of hands over me, and thrusting of
　　fingers through my hair and beard;
From the long sustained kiss upon the mouth or bosom;
From the close pressure that makes me or any man drunk,
　　fainting with excess;
From what the divine husband knows – from the work of
　　fatherhood;
From exultation, victory, and relief – from the bedfellow's
　　embrace in the night;
From the act-poems of eyes, hands, hips, and bosoms,
From the cling of the trembling arm,
From the bending curve and the clinch,
From side by side, the pliant coverlid off-throwing,
From the one so unwilling to have me leave – and me just
　　as unwilling to leave,
(Yet a moment, O tender waiter, and I return;)
– From the hour of shining stars and dropping dews,
From the night, a moment, I, emerging, flitting out,
Celebrate you, act divine – and you, children prepared for,
And you, stalwart loins.

A. D. Hope

THE GATEWAY

Now the heart sings with all its thousand voices
To hear this city of cells, my body, sing.
The tree through the stiff clay at long last forces
Its thin strong roots and taps the secret spring.

And the sweet waters without intermission
Climb to the tips of its green tenement;
The breasts have borne the grace of their possession,
The lips have felt the pressure of content.

Here I come home: in this expected country
They know my name and speak it with delight.
I am the dream and you my gates of entry,
The means by which I waken into light.

Stephen Spender

DAYBREAK

At dawn she lay with her profile at that angle
Which, when she sleeps, seems the carved face of an angel.
Her hair a harp, the hand of a breeze follows
And plays, against the white cloud of the pillows.
Then, in a flush of rose, she woke, and her eyes that opened
Swam in blue through her rose flesh that dawned.
From her dew of lips, the drop of one word
Fell like the first of fountains: murmured
'Darling', upon my ears the song of the first bird.

'My dream becomes my dream,' she said, 'come true.
I waken from you to my dream of you.'
Oh, my own wakened dream then dared assume
The audacity of her sleep. Our dreams
Poured into each other's arms, like streams.

Richard Brinsley Sheridan

THE GERANIUM

In the close covert of a grove,
By nature formed for scenes of love,
Said Susan in a lucky hour,
Observe yon sweet geranium flower;
How straight upon its stalk it stands,
And tempts our violating hands:
Whilst the soft bud as yet unspread,
Hangs down its pale declining head:
Yet, soon as it is ripe to blow,
The stems shall rise, the head shall glow.
Nature, said I, my lovely Sue,
To all her followers lends a clue;
Her simple laws themselves explain,
As links of one continued chain;
For her the mysteries of creation,
Are but the works of generation:
Yon blushing, strong, triumphant flower,
Is in the crisis of its power:
But short, alas! its vigorous reign,
He sheds his seed, and drops again;
The bud that hangs in pale decay,
Feels, not, as yet, the plastic ray;
Tomorrow's sun shall bid him rise,
Then, too, he sheds his seed and dies:

But words, my love, are vain and weak,
For proof, let bright example speak;
Then straight before the wondering maid,
The tree of life I gently laid;
Observe, sweet Sue, his drooping head,
How pale, how languid, and how dead;
Yet, let the sun of thy bright eyes,
Shine but a moment, it shall rise;
Let but the dew of thy soft hand
Refresh the stem, it straight shall stand:
Already, see, it swells, it grows,
Its head is redder than the rose,
Its shrivelled fruit, of dusky hue,
Now glows, a present fit for Sue:
The balm of life each artery fills,
And in o'erflowing drops distils.
Oh me! cried Susan, when is this?
What strange tumultuous throbs of bliss!
Sure, never mortal, till this hour,
Felt such emotion at a flower:
Oh, serpent! cunning to deceive,
Sure, 'tis this tree that tempted Eve;
The crimson apples hang so fair,
Alas! what woman could forbear?
Well hast thou guessed, my love, I cried,
It is the tree by which she died;
The tree which could content her,
All nature, Susan, seeks the centre;
Yet, let us still, poor Eve forgive,
It's the tree by which we live;
For lovely woman still it grows,
And in the centre only blows.
But chief for thee, it spreads its charms,
For paradise is in thy arms. —

I ceased, for nature kindly here
Began to whisper in her ear:
And lovely Sue lay softly panting,
While the geranium tree was planting.
'Til in the heat of amorous strife,
She burst the mellow tree of life.
'Oh, heaven!' cried Susan, with a sigh,
'The hour we taste — we surely die;
Strange raptures seize my fainting frame,
And all my body glows with flame;
Yet let me snatch one parting kiss
To tell my love I die with bliss:
That pleased, thy Susan yields her breath;
Oh! who would live if this be death!'

Abraham Cowley

DIALOGUE

AFTER ENJOYMENT

SHE. What have we done? what cruel passion moved thee,
    Thus to ruin her that loved thee?
   Me thou hast robbed, but what art thou
   Thyself the richer now?
    Shame succeeds the short-lived pleasure;
So soon is spent, and gone, this thy ill-gotten treasure.

HE. We have done no harm; nor was it theft in me,
    But noblest charity in thee.
   I'll the well-gotten pleasure
   Safe in my memory treasure;
    What though the flower itself do waste,
The essence from it drawn does long and sweeter last.

SHE. No: I'm undone; my honour thou hast slain,
  And nothing can restore't again.
  Art and labour to bestow,
  Upon the carcase of it now,
   Is but t'embalm a body dead,
 The figure may remain, the life and beauty's fled.

HE. Never, my dear, was honour yet undone,
  By love, but indiscretion.
  To the wise it all things does allow;
  And cares not what we do; but how.
   Like tapers shut in ancient urns,
 Unless it let in air, forever shines and burns.

SHE. Thou first perhaps who did'st the fault commit,
  Wilt make thy wicked boast of it.
  For men, with Roman pride, above
  The conquest, do the triumph love:
   Nor think a perfect victory gained,
 Unless they through the streets their captive lead
    enchained.

HE. Whoe'er his secret joys has open laid,
  The baud to his own wife is made.
  Beside what boast is left for me,
  Whose whole wealth's a gift from thee?
   'Tis you the conqueror are, 'tis you
 Who have not only ta'ne, but bound, and gagged me too.

SHE. Though public punishment we escape, the sin
  Will rack and torture us within:
  Guilt and sin our bosom bears;
  And though fair, yet the fruit appears,
   That worm which now the core does waste
 When long't has gnawed within will break the skin at
    last.

HE. That thirsty drink, that hungry food I sought,
    That wounded balm, is all my fault.
  And thou in pity didst apply,
  The kind and only remedy:
    The cause absolves the crime; since me
So mighty force did move, so mighty goodness thee.

SHE. Curse on thine arts! methinks I hate thee now;
    And yet I'm sure I love thee too!
  I'm angry, but my wrath will prove,
  More innocent than did thy love.
    Thou hast this day undone me quite;
Yet wilt undo me more should'st thou not come at night.

Sir Charles Sedley

ON THE HAPPY CORYDON AND PHYLLIS

    Young Corydon and Phyllis
      Sat in a lovely grove,
    Contriving crowns of lilies,
      Repeating toys of love,
    And something else, but what I dare not name.

    But as they were a-playing,
      She ogled so the swain;
    It saved her plainly saying
      Let's kiss to ease our pain:
    And something else, but what I dare not name.

    A thousand times he kissed her,
      Laying her on the green;
    But as he farther pressed her,
      A pretty leg was seen:
    And something else, but what I dare not name.

So many beauties viewing,
   His ardour still increased;
And greater joys pursuing,
   He wandered o'er her breast:
And something else, but what I dare not name.

A last effort she trying,
   His passion to withstand;
Cried, but it was faintly crying,
   Pray take away your hand:
And something else, but what I dare not name.

Young Corydon grown bolder,
   The minutes would improve;
This is the time, he told her,
   To show you how I love;
And something else, but what I dare not name.

The nymph seemed almost dying,
   Dissolved in amorous heat;
She kissed and told him sighing,
   My dear your love is great:
And something else, but what I dare not name.

But Phyllis did recover
   Much sooner than the swain;
She blushing asked her lover,
   Shall we not kiss again:
And something else, but what I dare not name.

Thus Love his revels keeping,
   'Til Nature at a stand;
From talk they fell to sleeping,
   Holding each others hand;
And something else, but what I dare not name.

Catullus

Phyllis Corydon clutched to him
her head at rest beneath his chin.
He said, 'If I don't love you more
than ever maid was loved before
I shall (if this the years not prove)
in Afric or the Indian grove
some green-eyed lion serve for food.'
  Amor, to show that he was pleased,
  approvingly (in silence) sneezed.
Then Phyllis slightly raised her head
(her lips were full & wet & red)
to kiss the sweet eyes full of her:
'Corydon mine, with me prefer
always to serve unique Amor:
my softer flesh the fire licks
more greedily and deeper sticks.'
  Amor, to show that he was pleased,
  approvingly (in silence) sneezed.
So loving & loved so, they rove
between twin auspices of Love.
Corydon sets in his eye-lust
Phyllis before all other dust;
Phyllis on Corydon expends
her nubile toys, Love's dividends.
Could Venus yield more love-delight
than here she grants in Love's requite?

Translated from the Latin
by Peter Whigham

145

Fleur Adcock

NOTE ON PROPERTIUS 1.5

Among the Roman love-poets, possession
Is a rare theme. The locked and flower-hung door,
The shivering lover, are allowed. To more
Buoyant moods, the canons of expression
Gave grudging sanction. Do we, then, assume,
Finding Propertius tear-sodden and jealous,
That Cynthia was inexorably callous?
Plenty of moonlight entered that high room
Whose doors had met his Alexandrine battles;
And she, so gay a lutanist, was known
To stitch and doze a night away, alone,
Until the poet tumbled in with apples
For penitence and for her head his wreath,
Brought from a party, of wine-scented roses –
(The garland's aptness lying, one supposes,
Less in the flowers than in the thorns beneath:
Her waking could, he knew, provide his verses
With less idyllic themes.) Onto her bed
He rolled the round fruit, and adorned her head;
Then gently roused her sleeping mouth to curses.
Here the conventions reassert their power:
The apples fall and bruise, the roses wither,
Touched by a sallowed moon. But there were other
Luminous nights – (even the cactus flower
Glows briefly golden, fed by spiny flesh) –
And once, as he acknowledged, all was singing:
The moonlight musical, the darkness clinging,
And she compliant to his every wish.

Richard Duke

After the fiercest pangs of hot desire,
   Between Panthea's rising breasts
   His bending head Philander rests,
Though vanquished, yet unknowing to retire,
   Close hugs the charmer, and, ashamed to yield,
   Though he has lost the day, still keeps the field.

When, with a sigh, the fair Panthea said,
   'What pity 'tis, ye gods, that all
   The bravest warriors soonest fall!'
Then, with a kiss, she gently raised his head,
   Armed him again for fight, for nobly she
   More loved the combat than the victory.

Then, more enraged for being beat before,
   With all his strength he does prepare
   More fiercely to renew the war;
Nor ceases till that noble prize he bore;
   Even her such wonderous courage did surprise;
   She hugs the dart that wounded her, and dies.

John Dryden

SONG

Whilst Alexis lay pressed
   In her arms he loved best,
With his hands round her neck,
   And his head on her breast,
He found the fierce pleasure too hasty to stay,
And his soul in the tempest just flying away.

When Celia saw this,
With a sigh and a kiss,
She cried, 'Oh, my dear, I am robbed of my bliss;
'Tis unkind to your love, and unfaithfully done,
To leave me behind you, and die all alone.'

The youth, though in haste,
And breathing his last,
In pity died slowly, while she died more fast;
Till at length she cried, 'Now, my dear, now let us go:
Now die, my Alexis, and I will die too.'

Thus entranced they did lie,
Till Alexis did try
To recover new breath, that again he might die:
Then often they died; but the more they did so,
The nymph died more quick, and the shepherd more slow.

E. E. Cummings

i like my body when it is with your
body. It is so quite new a thing.
Muscles better and nerves more.
i like your body. i like what it does,
i like its hows. i like to feel the spine
of your body and its bones, and the trembling
-firm-smooth ness and which i will
again and again and again
kiss, i like kissing this and that of you,
i like, slowly stroking the, shocking fuzz
of your electric fur, and what-is-it comes
over parting flesh . . . . And eyes big love-crumbs,

and possibly i like the thrill

of under me you so quite new

John Donne

THE ECSTASY

Where, like a pillow on a bed,
   A pregnant bank swelled up, to rest
The violet's reclining head,
   Sat we two, one another's best.

Our hands were firmly cemented
   With a fast balm, which thence did spring;
Our eye-beams twisted, and did thread
   Our eyes upon one double string;

So to entergraft our hands, as yet
   Was all our means to make us one.
And pictures on our eyes to get
   Was all our propagation.

As 'twixt two equal armies, Fate
   Suspends uncertain victory,
Our souls (which to advance their state
   Were gone out) hung 'twixt her and me.

And whilst our souls negotiate there,
   We like sepulchral statues lay;
All day the same our postures were,
   And we said nothing all the day.

If any, so by love refined
   That he soul's language understood,
And by good love were grown all mind,
   Within convenient distance stood,

149

He (though he knew not which soul spake,
    Because both meant, both spake the same)
Might thence a new concoction take,
    And part far purer than he came.

This ecstasy doth unperplex
    (We said) and tell us what we love,
We see by this, it was not sex,
    We see, we saw not what did move:

But as all several souls contain
    Mixture of things, they know not what,
Love these mixed souls doth mix again,
    And makes both one, each this and that.

A single violet transplant,
    The strength, the colour, and the size,
(All which before was poor and scant)
    Redoubles still, and multiplies.

When love with one another so
    Interinanimates two souls,
That abler soul, which thence doth flow,
    Defects of loneliness controls.

We then, who are this new soul, know
    Of what we are composed, and made,
For the atomies of which we grow
    Are souls, whom no change can invade.

But, O alas! so long, so far
    Our bodies why do we forbear?
They are ours, though they are not we; we are
    The intelligences, they the sphere.

We owe them thanks, because they thus
    Did us, to us, at first convey,
Yielded their forces, sense, to us,
    Nor are dross to us, but allay.

On man heaven's influence works not so,
    But that it first imprints the air;
So soul into the soul may flow,
    Though it to body first repair.

As our blood labours to beget
    Spirits, as like souls as it can;
Because such fingers need to knit
    That subtle knot, which makes us man;

So must pure lovers' souls descend
    To affections, and to faculties,
Which sense may reach and apprehend,
    Else a great Prince in prison lies.

To our bodies turn we then, that so
    Weak men on love revealed may look;
Love's mysteries in souls do grow,
    But yet the body is his book.

And if some lover, such as we,
    Have heard this dialogue of one,
Let him still mark us, he shall see
    Small change, when we're to bodies gone.

William Davenant

UNDER THE WILLOW-SHADES

Under the willow-shades they were
   Free from the eye-sight of the sun,
For no intruding beam could there
   Peep through to spy what things were done:
     Thus sheltered they unseen did lie,
     Surfeiting on each other's eye;
Defended by the willow-shades alone,
The sun's heat they defied and cooled their own.

Whilst they did embrace unspied,
   The conscious willow seemed to smile,
That them with privacy supplied,
   Holding the door, as 't were, the while;
     And when their dalliances were o'er,
     The willows, to oblige them more,
Bowing, did seem to say, as they withdrew,
'We can supply you with a cradle too.'

Boris Pasternak

HOPS

Beneath the willow wound round with ivy
we take cover from the worst
of the storm, with a greatcoat round
our shoulders and my hands around your waist.

152

I've got it wrong. That isn't ivy
entwined in the bushes round
the wood, but hops. You intoxicate me!
Let's spread the greatcoat on the ground.

Translated from the Russian by
Jon Stallworthy and Peter France

W. R. Rodgers

THE NET

Quick, woman, in your net
Catch the silver I fling!
O I am deep in your debt,
Draw tight, skin-tight, the string,
And rake the silver in.
No fisher ever yet
Drew such a cunning ring.

Ah, shifty as the fin
Of any fish this flesh
That, shaken to the shin,
Now shoals into your mesh,
Bursting to be held in;
Purse-proud and pebble-hard,
Its pence like shingle showered.

Open the haul, and shake
The fill of shillings free,
Let all the satchels break
And leap about the knee
In shoals of ecstasy.
Guineas and gills will flake
At each gull-plunge of me.

Though all the Angels, and
Saint Michael at their head,
Nightly contrive to stand
On guard about your bed,
Yet none dare take a hand,
But each can only spread
His eagle-eye instead.

But I, being man, can kiss
And bed-spread-eagle too;
All flesh shall come to this,
Being less than angel is,
Yet higher far in bliss
As it entwines with you.
Come, make no sound, my sweet;
Turn down the candid lamp
And draw the equal quilt
Over our naked guilt.

Algernon Charles Swinburne

LOVE AND SLEEP

Lying asleep between the strokes of night
  I saw my love lean over my sad bed,
  Pale as the duskiest lily's leaf or head,
Smooth-skinned and dark, with bare throat made to bite,
Too wan for blushing and too warm for white,
  But perfect-coloured without white or red.
  And her lips opened amorously, and said –
I wist not what, saving one word – Delight.

And all her face was honey to my mouth,
   And all her body pasture to mine eyes;
      The long lithe arms and hotter hands than fire,
The quivering flanks, hair smelling of the south,
   The bright light feet, the splendid supple thighs
      And glittering eyelids of my soul's desire.

W. H. Auden

Lay your sleeping head, my love,
Human on my faithless arm;
Time and fevers burn away
Individual beauty from
Thoughtful children, and the grave
Proves the child ephemeral:
But in my arms till break of day
Let the living creature lie,
Mortal, guilty, but to me
The entirely beautiful.

Soul and body have no bounds:
To lovers as they lie upon
Her tolerant enchanted slope
In their ordinary swoon,
Grave the vision Venus sends
Of supernatural sympathy,
Universal love and hope;
While an abstract insight wakes
Among the glaciers and the rocks
The hermit's sensual ecstasy.

Certainty, fidelity
On the stroke of midnight pass
Like vibrations of a bell
And fashionable madmen raise
Their pedantic boring cry;
Every farthing of the cost,
All the dreaded cards foretell,
Shall be paid, but from this night
Not a whisper, not a thought,
Not a kiss nor look be lost.

Beauty, midnight, vision dies:
Let the winds of dawn that blow
Softly round your dreaming head
Such a day of sweetness show
Eye and knocking heart may bless,
Find the mortal world enough;
Noons of dryness see you fed
By the involuntary powers,
Nights of insult let you pass
Watched by every human love.

W. B. Yeats

LULLABY

Beloved, may your sleep be sound
That have found it where you fed.
What were all the world's alarms
To mighty Paris when he found
Sleep upon a golden bed
That first dawn in Helen's arms?

Sleep, beloved, such a sleep
As did that wild Tristram know
When, the potion's work being done,
Roe could run or doe could leap
Under oak and beechen bough,
Roe could leap or doe could run;

Such a sleep and sound as fell
Upon Eurotas' grassy bank
When the holy bird, that there
Accomplished his predestined will,
From the limbs of Leda sank
But not from her protecting care.

Alan Ross

IN BLOEMFONTEIN

Woman to man, they lie,
He not quite white
As she, nor she
So black as he.

Save where her stomach curves
His flesh and hers,
Commingling, match.
Eyes catch,

That dare not meet
Beyond the night,
Though their alternate
Thighs, locked tight,

Defy you to discriminate
Between his skin and hers.
To him Pass Laws
Apply; she knows no night.

But that pale strip her loins
Keep from the sun
Marks her, his tiger-woman,
White, while he's all one.

That strip convicts. He covers
With his hand the site
Of crime. Soon shutters,
Striping him with light

Peel colour from his hips –
She his woman, he
Her man, simply human
Like the heart beneath her lips.

A matter of degree
Elsewhere, no more;
But here, in Bloemfontein,
Keep closed the door.

Robert Graves

SHE TELLS HER LOVE WHILE HALF ASLEEP

She tells her love while half asleep,
   In the dark hours,
     With half-words whispered low:
As Earth stirs in her winter sleep
   And puts out grass and flowers
     Despite the snow,
     Despite the falling snow.

Elizabeth Jennings

WINTER LOVE

Let us have winter loving that the heart
May be in peace and ready to partake
Of the slow pleasure spring would wish to hurry
Or that in summer harshly would awake,
And let us fall apart, O gladly weary,
The white skin shaken like a white snowflake.

John Donne

THE SUN RISING

Busy old fool, unruly Sun,
    Why dost thou thus,
Through windows and through curtains call on us?
Must to thy motions lovers' seasons run?
    Saucy pedantic wretch, go chide
    Late school-boys, and sour 'prentices,
  Go tell court-huntsmen that the King will ride,
  Call country ants to harvest offices;
Love, all alike, no season knows, nor clime,
Nor hours, days, months, which are the rags of time.

    Thy beams, so reverend and strong
        Why shouldst thou think?
I could eclipse and cloud them with a wink,
But that I would not lose her sight so long:

If her eyes have not blinded thine,
Look, and tomorrow late tell me,
Whether both the Indias of spice and mine
Be where thou left'st them, or lie here with me.
Ask for those kings whom thou saw'st yesterday,
And thou shalt hear, 'All here in one bed lay.'

She's all States, and all Princes I;
Nothing else is.
Princes do but play us; compared to this,
All honour's mimic; all wealth alchemy.
Thou, Sun, art half as happy as we,
In that the world's contracted thus;
Thine age asks ease, and since thy duties be
To warm the world, that's done in warming us.
Shine here to us, and thou art everywhere;
This bed thy centre is, these walls thy sphere.

John Donne

THE GOOD MORROW

I wonder by my troth, what thou and I
Did, till we loved? were we not weaned till then?
But sucked on country pleasures, childishly?
Or snorted we i'the seven sleepers' den?
'Twas so; But this, all pleasures fancies be.
If ever any beauty I did see,
Which I desired, and got, 'twas but a dream of thee.

And now good morrow to our waking souls,
Which watch not one another out of fear;
For love, all love of other sights controls,
And makes one little room, an everywhere.

Let sea-discoverers to new worlds have gone,
   Let maps to others, worlds on worlds have shown,
Let us possess our world, each hath one, and is one.

   My face in thine eye, thine in mine appears,
      And true plain hearts do in the faces rest,
   Where can we find two better hemispheres
      Without sharp North, without declining West?
   Whatever dies, was not mixed equally;
      If our two loves be one, or, thou and I
Love so alike, that none do slacken, none can die.

Jacques Prévert
ALICANTE

An orange on the table
Your dress on the rug
   And you in my bed
Sweet present of the present
   Cool of night
   Warmth of my life.

*Translated from the French by
Lawrence Ferlinghetti*

W. H. Auden

Fish in the unruffled lakes
The swarming colours wear,
Swans in the winter air
A white perfection have,
And the great lion walks
Through his innocent grove;
Lion, fish, and swan
Act, and are gone
Upon Time's toppling wave.

We till shadowed days are done,
We must weep and sing
Duty's conscious wrong,
The Devil in the clock,
The Goodness carefully worn
For atonement or for luck;
We must lose our loves,
On each beast and bird that moves
Turn an envious look.

Sighs for folly said and done
Twist our narrow days;
But I must bless, I must praise
That you, my swan, who have
All gifts that to the swan
Impulsive Nature gave,
The majesty and pride,
Last night should add
Your voluntary love.

John Heath-Stubbs

THE UNPREDICTED

The goddess Fortune be praised (on her toothed wheel
I have been mincemeat these several years)
Last night, for a whole night, the unpredictable
Lay in my arms, in a tender and unquiet rest —
(I perceived the irrelevance of my former tears) —
Lay, and at dawn departed. I rose and walked the streets
Where a whitsuntide wind blew fresh, and blackbirds
Incontestably sang, and the people were beautiful.

Petronius Arbiter

Good God, what a night that was,
The bed was so soft, and how we clung,
Burning together, lying this way and that,
Our uncontrollable passions
Flowing through our mouths.
If I could only die that way,
I'd say goodbye to the business of living.

*Translated from the Greek by
Kenneth Rexroth*

Lawrence Durrell

THIS UNIMPORTANT MORNING

This unimportant morning
Something goes singing where
The capes turn over on their sides
And the warm Adriatic rides
Her blue and sun washing
At the edge of the world and its brilliant cliffs.

Day rings in the higher airs
Pure with cicadas, and slowing
Like a pulse to smoke from farms,
Extinguished in the exhausted earth,
Unclenching like a fist and going.

Trees fume, cool, pour — and overflowing
Unstretch the feathers of birds and shake
Carpets from windows, brush with dew
The up-and-doing: and young lovers now
Their little resurrections make.

And now lightly to kiss all whom sleep
Stitched up — and wake, my darling, wake.
The impatient Boatman has been waiting
Under the house, his long oars folded up
Like wings in waiting on the darkling lake.

Robert Graves

THE QUIET GLADES OF EDEN

All such proclivities are tabulated —
By trained pathologists, in detail too —
The obscener parts of speech compulsively
Shrouded in Classic Latin.

But though my pleasure in your feet and hair
Is ungainsayable, let me protest
(Dear love) I am no trichomaniac
And no foot-fetichist.

If it should please you, for your own best reasons,
To take and flog me with a rawhide whip,
I might (who knows?) surprisedly accept
This earnest of affection.

Nothing, agreed, is alien to love
When pure desire has overflowed its baulks;
But why must private sportiveness be viewed
Through public spectacles?

Enough, I will not claim a heart unfluttered
By these case-histories of aberrancy;
Nevertheless a long cool draught of water,
Or a long swim in the bay,

Serves to restore my wholesome appetite
For you and what we do at night together:
Which is no more than Adam did with Eve
In the quiet glades of Eden.

Lawrence Ferlinghetti

AWAY ABOVE A HARBORFUL

Away above a harborful
                    of caulkless houses
among the charley noble chimneypots
                    of a rooftop rigged with clotheslines
    a woman pastes up sails
                    upon the wind
hanging out her morning sheets
                    with wooden pins
            O lovely mamma!
                    her nearly naked teats
        throw taut shadows
                when she stretches up
to hang at last the last of her
                so white washed sins
        but it is wetly amorous
                and winds itself about her
        clinging to her skin
                So caught with arms upraised
    she tosses back her head
                in voiceless laughter
and in choiceless gesture then
                    shakes out gold hair
while in the reachless seascape spaces
                    between the blown white shrouds
    stand out the bright steamers
                to kingdom come

Harry Fainlight

A BRIDE

In bed with the stranger who had picked him up,
He lies awake in the dark;
How calmly happy he is feeling.

Thrown by the pattern of holes in the top
Of an old-fashioned paraffin stove, a magic
Cathedral window glows on the ceiling.

* * *

Hollow-feeling, empty of sleep and as yet unbreakfasted,
From an already forgotten stranger's bed
I stumble out into an unfamiliar part of the town.

So dazzlingly greeted! The sunlight's sudden recognition
  breaking
Across a row of houses I have never seen;
These shoppers remote as if some distant generation.

World, empty of me as I am of you now,
Let me ask of you nothing.
All now seems possible. O let me nothing ask.

C. P. Cavafy

ON THE STREET

His compassionate face, slightly wan;
his chestnut eyes, as if ringed;
he is twenty-five years old, but looks more like twenty;
with something artistic in his dress,
— a touch of colour in his tie, a bit of shape to his collar —
he walks aimlessly on the street,
as if hypnotized still by the deviate sensual delight,
by the so deviate sensual delight he has enjoyed.

*Translated from the Greek by
Rae Dalven*

Robert Creeley

THE WAY

My love's manners in bed
are not to be discussed by me,
as mine by her
I would not credit comment upon gracefully.

Yet I ride by the margin of that lake in
the wood, the castle,
and the excitement of strongholds;
and have a small boy's notion of doing good.

Oh well, I will say here,
knowing each man,
let you find a good wife too,
and love her as hard as you can.

Robert Lowell

MAN AND WIFE

Tamed by Miltown, we lie on Mother's bed;
the rising sun in war paint dyes us red;
in broad daylight her gilded bed-posts shine,
abandoned, almost Dionysian.
At last the trees are green on Marlborough Street,
blossoms on our magnolia ignite
the morning with their murderous five days' white.
All night I've held your hand,
as if you had
a fourth time faced the kingdom of the mad –
its hackneyed speech, its homicidal eye –
and dragged me home alive. . . . Oh my *Petite*,
clearest of all God's creatures, still all air and nerve:
you were in your twenties, and I,
once hand on glass
and heart in mouth,
outdrank the Rahvs in the heat
of Greenwich Village, fainting at your feet –
too boiled and shy
and poker-faced to make a pass,
while the shrill verve
of your invective scorched the traditional South.

Now twelve years later, you turn your back.
Sleepless, you hold
your pillow to your hollows like a child,
your old-fashioned tirade –
loving, rapid, merciless –
breaks like the Atlantic Ocean on my head.

Sir John Harington

THE AUTHOR TO HIS WIFE,
OF A WOMAN'S ELOQUENCE

My Mall, I mark that when you mean to prove me
To buy a velvet gown, or some rich border,
Thou call'st me good sweet heart, thou swear'st to love me,
Thy locks, thy lips, thy looks, speak all in order,
Thou think'st, and right thou think'st, that these do move
    me,
That all these severally thy suit do further:
    But shall I tell thee what most thy suit advances?
    Thy fair smooth words? no, no, thy fair smooth
      haunches.

Anon

SEVENTEENTH CENTURY
MADRIGAL

My Love in her attire doth show her wit,
    It doth so well become her;
For every season she hath dressings fit,
    For Winter, Spring, and Summer.
      No beauty she doth miss
        When all her robes are on:
      But Beauty's self she is
        When all her robes are gone.

Octavio Paz

TOUCH

My hands
Open the curtains of your being
Clothe you in a further nudity
Uncover the bodies of your body
My hands
Invent another body for your body

*Translated from the Spanish by
Charles Tomlinson*

Charles Baudelaire

THE JEWELS

My well-beloved was stripped. Knowing my whim,
She wore her tinkling gems, but naught besides:
And showed such pride as, while her luck betides,
A sultan's favoured slave may show to him.

When it lets off its lively, crackling sound,
This blazing blend of metal crossed with stone,
Gives me an ecstasy I've only known
Where league of sound and lustre can be found.

She let herself be loved: then, drowsy-eyed,
Smiled down from her high couch in languid ease.
My love was deep and gentle as the seas
And rose to her as to a cliff the tide.

My own approval of each dreamy pose,
Like a tamed tiger, cunningly she sighted:
And candour, with lubricity united,
Gave piquancy to every one she chose.

Her limbs and hips, burnished with changing lustres,
Before my eyes clairvoyant and serene,
Swanned themselves, undulating in their sheen;
Her breasts and belly, of my vine the clusters,

Like evil angels rose, my fancy twitting,
To kill the peace which over me she'd thrown,
And to disturb her from the crystal throne
Where, calm and solitary, she was sitting.

So swerved her pelvis that, in one design,
Antiope's white rump it seemed to graft
To a boy's torso, merging fore and aft.
The talc on her brown tan seemed half-divine.

The lamp resigned its dying flame. Within,
The hearth alone lit up the darkened air,
And every time it sighed a crimson flare
It drowned in blood that amber-coloured skin.

*Translated from the French by
Roy Campbell*

J. M. Synge

DREAD

Beside a chapel I'd a room looked down,
Where all the women from the farms and town,
On Holy-days, and Sundays used to pass
To marriages, and Christenings and to Mass.

Then I sat lonely watching score and score,
Till I turned jealous of the Lord next door. . .
Now by this window, where there's none can see,
The Lord God's jealous of yourself and me.

Ted Hughes

SEPTEMBER

We sit late, watching the dark slowly unfold:
No clock counts this.
When kisses are repeated and the arms hold
There is no telling where time is.

It is midsummer: the leaves hang big and still:
Behind the eye a star,
Under the silk of the wrist a sea, tell
Time is nowhere.

We stand; leaves have not timed the summer.
No clock now needs
Tell we have only what we remember:
Minutes uproaring with our heads

Like an unfortunate King's and his Queen's
When the senseless mob rules;
And quietly the trees casting their crowns
Into the pools.

Guillaume Apollinaire

THE MIRABEAU BRIDGE

Under the Mirabeau bridge the Seine
    Flows with our loves;
Must I remember once again
Joy followed always after pain?
    Night may come and clock may sound,
    Within your shadow I am bound.

Clasp hand in hand, keep face to face,
    Whilst here below
The bridge formed by our arms' embrace
The waters of our endless longing pass.
    Night may come and clock may sound,
    Within your shadow I am bound.

And like this stream our passions flow,
    Our love goes by;
The violence hope dare not show
Follows time's beat which now falls slow.
    Night may come and clock may sound,
    Within your shadow I am bound.

The days move on; but still we strain
    Back towards time past;
Still to the waters of the Seine
We bend to catch the echo gone.
    Night may come and clock may sound,
    Within your shadow I am bound.

Translated from the French by
Quentin Stevenson

173

Andrei Voznesensky

DEAD STILL

Now, with your palms on the blades of my shoulders,
Let us embrace:
Let there be only your lips' breath on my face,
Only, behind our backs, the plunge of rollers.

Our backs, which like two shells in moonlight shine,
Are shut behind us now;
We lie here huddled, listening brow to brow,
Like life's twin formula or double sign.

In folly's world-wide wind
Our shoulders shield from the weather
The calm we now beget together,
Like a flame held between hand and hand.

Does each cell have a soul within it?
If so, fling open all your little doors,
And all your souls shall flutter like the linnet
In the cages of my pores.

Nothing is hidden that shall not be known.
Yet by no storm of scorn shall we
Be pried from this embrace, and left alone
Like muted shells forgetful of the sea.

Meanwhile, O load of stress and bother,
Lie on the shells of our backs in a great heap:
It will but press us closer, one to the other.

We are asleep.

*Translated from the Russian by
Richard Wilbur*

E. E. Cummings

somewhere i have never travelled, gladly beyond
any experience, your eyes have their silence:
in your most frail gesture are things which enclose me.
or which i cannot touch because they are too near

your slightest look easily will unclose me
though i have closed myself as fingers,
you open always petal by petal myself as Spring opens
(touching skilfully, mysteriously) her first rose

or if your wish be to close me, i and
my life will shut very beautifully, suddenly,
as when the heart of this flower imagines
the snow carefully everywhere descending;

nothing which we are to perceive in this world equals
the power of your intense fragility: whose texture
compels me with the colour of its countries,
rendering death and forever with each breathing

(i do not know what it is about you that closes
and opens; only something in me understands
the voice of your eyes is deeper than all roses)
nobody, not even the rain, has such small hands

Sir Thomas Wyatt

Once as methought Fortune me kissed
    And bad me ask what I thought best;
And I should have it as me list,
    Therewith to set my heart in rest.

175

I askèd but my Lady's heart
    To have for evermore mine own:
Then at an end were all my smart,
    Then I should need no more to moan.

Yet for all that a stormy blast
    Had overturned this goodly day;
And Fortune seemèd at the last
    That to her promise she said nay.

But like as one out of despair
    To sudden hope revivèd I;
Now Fortune showeth herself so fair
    That I content me wonderly.

My most desire my hand may reach,
    My will is always at my hand;
Me need not long for to beseech
    Her that hath power me to command.

What earthly thing more can I crave?
    What would I wish more at my will?
Nothing on earth more would I have,
    Save that I have to have it still.

For Fortune now hath kept her promise
    In granting me my most desire:
Of my sufferance I have redress,
    And I content me with my hire.

Sir Philip Sidney

My true love hath my heart, and I have his,
By just exchange, one for the other given.
I hold his dear, and mine he cannot miss:
There never was a better bargain driven.
His heart in me, keeps me and him in one,
My heart in him, his thoughts and senses guides:
He loves my heart, for once it was his own:
I cherish his, because in me it bides.
His heart his wound receivèd from my sight:
My heart was wounded with his wounded heart,
For as from me, on him his hurt did light,
So still methought in me his hurt did smart:
　　Both equal hurt, in this change sought our bliss:
　　My true love hath my heart and I have his.

Edwin Muir

IN LOVE FOR LONG

I've been in love for long
With what I cannot tell
And will contrive a song
For the intangible
That has no mould or shape,
From which there's no escape.

It is not even a name,
Yet is all constancy;
Tried or untried, the same,
It cannot part from me;
A breath, yet as still
As the established hill.

It is not any thing,
And yet all being is;
Being, being, being,
Its burden and its bliss.
How can I ever prove
What it is I love?

This happy happy love
Is sieged with crying sorrows,
Crushed beneath and above
Between todays and morrows;
A little paradise
Held in the world's vice.

And there it is content
And careless as a child,
And in imprisonment
Flourishes sweet and wild;
In wrong, beyond wrong,
All the world's day long.

This love a moment known
For what I do not know
And in a moment gone
Is like the happy doe
That keeps its perfect laws
Between the tiger's paws
And vindicates its cause.

AN HOUR WITH THEE

An hour with thee! When earliest day
Dapples with gold the eastern grey,
Oh, what can frame my mind to bear
The toil and turmoil, cark and care,
New griefs, which coming hours unfold,
And sad remembrance of the old?
        One hour with thee.

One hour with thee! When burning June
Waves his red flag at pitch of noon;
What shall repay the faithful swain,
His labour on the sultry plain;
And, more than cave or sheltering bough,
Cool feverish blood and throbbing brow?
        One hour with thee.

One hour with thee! When sun is set,
Oh, what can teach me to forget
The thankless labours of the day;
The hopes, the wishes, flung away;
The increasing wants, and lessening gains,
The master's pride, who scorns my pains?
        One hour with thee.

John Donne

THE ANNIVERSARY

All Kings, and all their favourites,
    All glory of honours, beauties, wits,
The sun itself, which makes times, as they pass,
Is elder by a year now than it was
When thou and I first one another saw:
All other things to their destruction draw,
    Only our love hath no decay;
This no tomorrow hath, nor yesterday,
Running it never runs from us away,
But truly keeps his first, last, everlasting day.

    Two graves must hide thine and my corse;
    If one might, death were no divorce.
Alas, as well as other Princes, we
(Who Prince enough in one another be)
Must leave at last in death these eyes and ears,
Oft fed with true oaths, and with sweet salt tears;
    But souls where nothing dwells but love
(All other thoughts being inmates) then shall prove
This, or a love increasèd there above,
When bodies to their graves, souls from their graves remove.

    And then we shall be throughly blessed;
    But we no more than all the rest.
Here upon earth we're Kings, and none but we
Can be such Kings, nor of such subjects be;
Who is so safe as we? where none can do
Treason to us, except one of us two.
    True and false fears let us refrain,
Let us love nobly, and live, and add again
Years and years unto years, till we attain
To write threescore: this is the second of our reign.

I KNEW A WOMAN

I knew a woman, lovely in her bones,
When small birds sighed, she would sigh back at them;
Ah, when she moved, she moved more ways than one:
The shapes a bright container can contain!
Of her choice virtues only gods should speak,
Or English poets who grew up on Greek
(I'd have them sing in chorus, cheek to cheek).

How well her wishes went! She stroked my chin,
She taught me Turn, and Counter-turn, and Stand;
She taught me Touch, that undulant white skin;
I nibbled meekly from her proffered hand;
She was the sickle; I, poor I, the rake,
Coming behind her for her pretty sake
(But what prodigious mowing we did make).

Love likes a gander, and adores a goose:
Her full lips pursed, the errant note to seize;
She played it quick, she played it light and loose;
My eyes, they dazzled at her flowing knees;
Her several parts could keep a pure repose,
Or one hip quiver with a mobile nose
(She moved in circles, and those circles moved).

Let seed be grass, and grass turn into hay:
I'm martyr to a motion not my own;
What's freedom for? To know eternity.
I swear she cast a shadow white as stone.
But who would count eternity in days?
These old bones live to learn her wanton ways:
(I measure time by how a body sways).

A SONG OF A YOUNG LADY TO HER ANCIENT LOVER

Ancient person, for whom I
All the flattering youth defy,
Long be it ere thou grow old,
Aching, shaking, crazy, cold;
    But still continue as thou art,
    Ancient person of my heart.

On thy withered lips and dry,
Which like barren furrows lie,
Brooding kisses I will pour
Shall thy youthful heat restore
(Such kind showers in autumn fall,
And a second spring recall);
    Nor from thee will ever part,
    Ancient person of my heart.

The nobler part, which but to name
In our sex would be counted shame,
By age's frozen grasp possessed,
From his ice shall be released,
And soothed by my reviving hand,
In former warmth and vigour stand.
All a lover's wish can reach
For thy joy my love shall teach,
And for thy pleasure shall improve
All that art can add to love.
    Yet still I love thee without art,
    Ancient person of my heart.

Lord Byron

So, we'll go no more a-roving
    So late into the night,
Though the heart be still as loving,
    And the moon be still as bright.

For the sword outwears its sheath,
    And the soul wears out the breast,
And the heart must pause to breathe,
    And love itself have rest.

Though the night was made for loving,
    And the day returns too soon,
Yet we'll go no more a-roving
    By the light of the moon.

Fyodor Tyutchev

LAST LOVE

Love at the closing of our days
is apprehensive and very tender.
Glow brighter, brighter, farewell rays
of one last love in its evening splendor.

Blue shade takes half the world away:
through western clouds alone some light is slanted.
O tarry, O tarry, declining day,
enchantment, let me stay enchanted.

183

The blood runs thinner, yet the heart
remains as ever deep and tender.
O last belated love, thou art
a blend of joy and of hopeless surrender.

Translated from the Russian by
Vladimir Nabokov

Robert Burns

JOHN ANDERSON MY JO

John Anderson my jo, John,
   When we were first acquent;
Your locks were like the raven,
   Your bony brow was brent;
But now your brow is beld, John,
   Your locks are like the snaw;
But blessings on your frosty pow,
   John Anderson my Jo.

John Anderson my jo, John,
   We clamb the hill the gither;
And mony a canty day, John,
   We've had wi' ane anither:
Now we maun totter down, John,
   And hand in hand we'll go;
And sleep the gither at the foot,
   John Anderson my Jo.

    pow head   *cantay* jolly

184

W. B. Yeats

A LAST CONFESSION

What lively lad most pleasured me
Of all that with me lay?
I answer that I gave my soul
And loved in misery,
But had great pleasure with a lad
That I loved bodily.

Flinging from his arms I laughed
To think his passion such
He fancied that I gave a soul
Did but our bodies touch,
And laughed upon his breast to think
Beast gave beast as much.

I gave what other women gave
That stepped out of their clothes,
But when this soul, its body off,
Naked to naked goes,
He it has found shall find therein
What none other knows,

And give his own and take his own
And rule in his own right;
And though it loved in misery
Close and cling so tight,
There's not a bird of day that dare
Extinguish that delight.

ABERRATIONS

William Congreve

SONG

Pious Selinda goes to prayers,
  If I but ask the favour;
And yet the tender fool's in tears,
  When she believes I'll leave her.

Would I were free from this restraint,
  Or else had hopes to win her;
Would she could make of me a saint,
  Or I of her a sinner.

Anon

SEVENTEENTH CENTURY

FRAGMENT OF A SONG ON THE BEAUTIFUL WIFE OF DR JOHN OVERALL, DEAN OF ST PAUL'S

The Dean of Paul's did search for his wife
  And where d'ee think he found her?
Even upon Sir John Selby's bed,
  As flat as any flounder.

OF AN HEROICAL ANSWER OF A GREAT ROMAN LADY TO HER HUSBAND

A grave wise man that had a great rich lady,
Such as perhaps in these days found there may be,
Did think she played him false and more than think,
Save that in wisdom he thereat did wink.
Howbeit one time disposed to sport and play
Thus to his wife he pleasantly did say,
'Since strangers lodge their arrows in thy quiver,
Dear dame, I pray you yet the cause deliver,
If you can tell the cause and not dissemble,
How all our children me so much resemble?'
The lady blushed but yet this answer made
'Though I have used some traffic in the trade,
And must confess, as you have touched before,
My bark was sometimes steered with foreign oar,
 Yet stowed I no man's stuff but first persuaded
 The bottom with your ballast full was laded.'

Federico García Lorca

THE FAITHLESS WIFE

And believing she was a maid,
I took her to the river,
but already she was married.

It was almost by agreement
upon Saint James's night.

190

The street-lamps went out
and the crickets lit up.
On the very last corner
I touched her sleeping breasts,
and like bouquets of hyacinth
they opened at once to my caress.
The starch of her petticoat
was sounding in my ears
like a piece of silk
that is rent by ten knives.
Without light on the tree-tops
the trees have grown huge
and far from the river
barks an horizon of dogs.

The brambles were passed,
the reeds and the furze.
Beneath the bun of her hair
I made a hollow in the earth.
I took off my tie,
she took off her dress.
I, my revolver-belt,
she her four bodices.
Not spikenard nor snail
have a skin so smooth,
nor do crystals shine
so brilliant in the moon.
Her thighs escaped from me
like two startled trout,
half full of cold
and half full of light.
By the best of all roads
that night I galloped
on a mother-of-pearl filly
without bridle or stirrups.

The things she said to me,
as a man, I won't repeat.
The light of understanding
has made me discreet.
I took her from the river
soiled with kisses and sand.
The swords of the lilies
fought with the wind.
A genuine gypsy,
I behaved as is proper,
and gave her a large work-box
of straw-coloured satin.
And I wished not to love her,
for though she was married,
she said she was a maiden
when I took her by the river.

*Translated from the Spanish by
A. L. Lloyd*

Abraham Cowley

HONOUR

She loves, and she confesses too;
There's then at last, no more to do.
The happy work's entirely done;
Enter the town which thou hast won;
The fruits of conquest now begin;
Iô triumph! Enter in.

What's this, ye Gods, what can it be?
Remains there still an enemy?
Bold honour stands up in the gate,
And would yet capitulate;
Have I o'recome all real foes,
And shall this phantom me oppose?

Noisy Nothing! stalking Shade!
By what witchcraft wert thou made?
Empty cause of solid harms!
But I shall find out counter-charms
Thy airy devilship to remove
From this circle here of love.

Sure I shall rid myself of thee
By the night's obscurity,
And obscurer secrecy.
Unlike to every other spright,
Thou attempt'st not men t'affright,
Nor appear'st but in the light.

John Wilmot, Earl of Rochester

THE IMPERFECT ENJOYMENT

Naked she lay; clasped in my longing arms,
I filled with love, and she all over charms;
Both equally inspired with eager fire,
Melting through kindness, flaming in desire.
With arms, legs, lips close clinging to embrace,
She clips me to her breast, and sucks me to her face.
Her nimble tongue, Love's lesser lightning, played
Within my mouth, and to my thoughts conveyed
Swift orders that I should prepare to throw
The all-dissolving thunderbolt below.
My fluttering soul, sprung with the pointed kiss,
Hangs hovering o'er her balmy brinks of bliss.
But whilst her busy hand would guide that part
Which should convey my soul up to her heart,
In liquid raptures I dissolve all o'er,
Melt into sperm, and spend at every pore.

A touch from any part of her had done 't:
Her hand, her foot, her very look's a cunt.

   Smiling, she chides in a kind murmuring noise,
And from her body wipes the clammy joys,
When, with a thousand kisses wandering o'er
My panting bosom, 'Is there then no more?'
She cries. 'All this to love and rapture's due;
Must we not pay a debt to pleasure too?'

   But I, the most forlorn, lost man alive,
To show my wished obedience vainly strive:
I sigh, alas! and kiss, but cannot swive.
Eager desires confound my first intent,
Succeeding shame does more success prevent,
And rage at last confirms me impotent.
Ev'n her fair hand, which might bid heat return
To frozen age, and make cold hermits burn,
Applied to my dead cinder, warms no more
Than fire to ashes could past flames restore.
Trembling, confused, despairing, limber, dry,
A wishing, weak, unmoving lump I lie.
This dart of love, whose piercing point, oft tried,
With virgin blood ten thousand maids have dyed;
Which nature still directed with such art
That it through every cunt reached every heart –
Stiffly resolved, 'twould carelessly invade
Woman or man, nor ought its fury stayed:
Where'er it pierced, a cunt it found or made –
Now languid lies in this unhappy hour,
Shrunk up and sapless like a withered flower.

   Thou treacherous, base deserter of my flame,
False to my passion, fatal to my fame,
Through what mistaken magic dost thou prove
So true to lewdness, so untrue to love?
What oyster-cinder-beggar-common whore
Did'st thou e'er fail in all thy life before?

When vice, disease, and scandal lead the way,
With what officious haste dost thou obey!
Like a rude, roaring hector in the streets
Who scuffles, cuffs, and justles all he meets,
But if his King or country claim his aid,
The rakehell villain shrinks and hides his head;
Ev'n so thy brutal valour is displayed,
Breaks every stew, does each small whore invade,
But when great Love the onset does command,
Base recreant to thy prince, thou dar'st not stand.
Worst part of me, and henceforth hated most,
Through all the town a common fucking post,
On whom each whore relieves her tingling cunt
As hogs on gates do rub themselves and grunt,
Mayst thou to ravenous chancres be a prey,
Or in consuming weepings waste away;
May strangury and stone thy days attend;
May'st thou ne'er piss, who didst refuse to spend
When all my joys did on false thee depend.
    And may ten thousand abler pricks agree
    To do the wronged Corinna right for thee.

limber limp
stew brothel
weepings discharges of moisture
  from the body

strangury slow and painful urina-
  tion
stone gallstone

Thomas Hardy

THE RUINED MAID

'O' Melia, my dear, this does everything crown!
Who could have supposed I should meet you in Town?
And whence such fair garments, such prosperi-ty?' –
'O didn't you know I'd been ruined?' said she.

–'You left us in tatters, without shoes or socks,
Tired of digging potatoes, and spudding up docks;
And now you've gay bracelets and bright feathers three!' –
'Yes: that's how we dress when we're ruined,' said she.

– 'At home in the barton you said "thee" and "thou,"
And "thik oon," and "theäs oon," and "t'other"; but now
Your talking quite fits 'ee for high compa-ny!' –
'Some polish is gained with one's ruin,' said she.

– 'Your hands were like paws then, your face blue and
    bleak
But now I'm bewitched by your delicate cheek,
And your little gloves fit as on any la-dy!' –
'We never do work when we're ruined,' said she.

– 'You used to call home-life a hag-ridden dream,
And you'd sigh, and you'd sock; but at present you seem
To know not of megrims or melancho-ly!' –
'True. One's pretty lively when ruined,' said she.

– 'I wish I had feathers, a fine sweeping gown,
And a delicate face, and could strut about Town!' –
'My dear – a raw country girl, such as you be,
Cannot quite expect that. You ain't ruined,' said she.

Thomas Randolph

PHYLLIS

Poor credulous and simple maid!
By what strange wiles art thou betrayed!
A treasure thou hast lost today
For which thou can'st no ransom pay.

How black art thou transformed with sin!
How strange a guilt gnaws me within!
Grief will convert this red to pale;
When every wake, and witsund-ale
Shall talk my shame; break, break sad heart
There is no medicine for my smart,
    No herb nor balm can cure my sorrow,
    Unless you meet again tomorrow.

Matthew Prior

CHASTE FLORIMEL

No – I'll endure ten thousand deaths,
    Ere any further I'll comply;
Oh! sir, no man on earth that breathes
    Had ever yet his hand so high!

Oh! take your sword, and pierce my heart,
    Undaunted see me meet the wound,
Oh! will you act a Tarquin's part?
    A second Lucrece you have found.

Thus to the pressing Corydon,
    Poor Florimel, unhappy maid!
Fearing by love to be undone,
    In broken dying accents said.

Delia, who held the conscious door,
    Inspired by truth and brandy, smiled,
Knowing that, sixteen months before,
    Our Lucrece had her second child.

197

And, hark ye! madam, cried the bawd,
　None of your flights, your high-rope dodging:
Be civil here, or march abroad;
　Oblige the squire, or quit the lodging.

Oh! have I – Florimel went on –
　Have I then lost my Delia's aid?
Where shall forsaken virtue run,
　If by her friends she is betrayed?

Oh! curse on empty friendship's name!
　Lord, what is all our future view!
Then, dear destroyer of my fame,
　Let my last succour be to you!

From Delia's rage, and Fortune's frown,
　A wretched love-sick maid deliver!
Oh! tip me but another crown,
　Dear sir, and make me yours for ever.

Alexander Pope

TWO OR THREE:
A RECIPE TO MAKE A CUCKOLD

Two or three visits, and two or three bows,
Two or three civil things, two or three vows,
Two or three kisses, with two or three sighs,
Two or three Jesus's – and let me dies –
Two or three squeezes, and two or three towses,
With two or three thousand pound lost at their houses,
Can never fail cuckolding two or three spouses.

towses tickles

198

Ovid

TO HIS MISTRESS

*whose husband is invited to a feast with them. The
poet instructs her how to behave herself in his company*

Your husband will be with us at the treat;
May that be the last supper he shall eat.
And am poor I, a guest invited there,
Only to see, while he may touch the Fair?
To see you kiss and hug your nauseous Lord,
While his lewd hand descends below the board?
Now wonder not that Hippodamia's charms,
At such a sight, the Centaurs urged to arms;
That in a rage they threw their cups aside,
Assailed the bridegroom, and would force the bride.
I am not half a horse (I would I were):
Yet hardly can from you my hands forbear.
Take then my counsel; which, observed, may be
Of some importance both to you and me.
Be sure to come before your man be there;
There's nothing can be done; but come howe'er.
Sit next him (that belongs to decency);
But tread upon my foot in passing by.
Read in my looks what silently they speak,
And slily, with your eyes, your answer make.
My lifted eyebrow shall declare my pain;
My right-hand to his fellow shall complain;
And on the back a letter shall design;
Besides a note that shall be writ in wine.
Whene'er you think upon our last embrace,
With your forefinger gently touch your face.

If any word of mine offend my dear,
Pull, with your hand, the velvet of your ear.
If you are pleased with what I do or say,
Handle your rings, or with your fingers play.
As suppliants use at altars, hold the board,
Whene'er you wish the Devil may take your Lord.
When he fills for you, never touch the cup;
But bid th' officious cuckold drink it up.
The waiter on those services employ.
Drink you, and I will snatch it from the boy:
Watching the part where your sweet mouth hath been,
And thence, with eager lips, will suck it in.
If he, with clownish manners, thinks it fit
To taste, and offer you the nasty bit,
Reject his greasy kindness, and restore
Th' unsavory morsel he had chewed before.
Nor let his arms embrace your neck, nor rest
Your tender cheek upon his hairy breast.
Let not his hand within your bosom stray,
And rudely with your pretty bubbies play.
But above all, let him no kiss receive;
That's an offence I never can forgive.
Do not, O do not that sweet mouth resign,
Lest I rise up in arms, and cry, 'Tis mine.
I shall thrust in betwixt, and void of fear
The manifest adulterer will appear.
These things are plain to sight; but more I doubt
What you conceal beneath your petticoat.
Take not his leg between your tender thighs,
Nor, with your hand, provoke my foe to rise.
How many love-inventions I deplore,
Which I, myself, have practised all before!

How oft have I been forced the robe to lift
In company to make a homely shift
For a bare bout, ill huddled o'er in haste,
While o'er my side the Fair her mantle cast.
You to your husband shall not be so kind;
But, lest you should, your mantle leave behind.
Encourage him to tope; but kiss him not,
Nor mix one drop of water in his pot.
If he be fuddled well, and snores apace
Then we may take advice from Time and Place.
When all depart, when compliments are loud,
Be sure to mix among the thickest crowd.
There I will be, and there we cannot miss,
Perhaps to grubble, or at least to kiss.
Alas, what length of labour I employ,
Just to secure a short and transient joy!
For night must part us; and when night is come,
Tucked underneath his arms he leads you home.
He locks you in; I follow to the door,
His fortune envy, and my own deplore.
He kisses you, he more than kisses too;
Th' outrageous cuckold thinks it all his due.
But, add not to his joy, by your consent,
And let it not be given, but only lent.
Return no kiss, nor move in any sort;
Make it a dull and a malignant sport.
Had I my wish, he should no pleasure take,
But slubber o'er your business for my sake.
And what e'er Fortune shall this night befall,
Coax me tomorrow, by forswearing all.

Translated from the Latin by
John Dryden

grubble grope   *slubber* hurry

Ezra Pound

THE TEMPERAMENTS

Nine adulteries, 12 liaisons, 64 fornications and something
    approaching a rape
Rest nightly upon the soul of our delicate friend Florialis,
And yet the man is so quiet and reserved in demeanour
That he passes for both bloodless and sexless.
Bastidides, on the contrary, who both talks and writes of
    nothing save copulation,
Has become the father of twins,
But he accomplished this feat at some cost;
He had to be four times cuckold.

John Berryman

Filling her compact & delicious body
with chicken páprika, she glanced at me
twice.
Fainting with interest, I hungered back
and only the fact of her husband & four other people
kept me from springing on her

or falling at her little feet and crying
'You are the hottest one for years of night
Henry's dazed eyes
have enjoyed, Brilliance.' I advanced upon
(despairing) my spumoni. – Sir Bones: is stuffed,
de world, wif feeding girls.

— Black hair, complexion Latin, jewelled eyes
downcast . . . The slob beside her feasts . . . What wonders is
she sitting on, over there?
The restaurant buzzes. She might as well be on Mars.
Where did it all go wrong? There ought to be a law against
   Henry.
— Mr Bones: there is.

Hilaire Belloc

JULIET

How did the party go in Portman Square?
I cannot tell you; Juliet was not there.

And how did Lady Gaster's party go?
Juliet was next me and I do not know.

John Press

WOMANISERS

Adulterers and customers of whores
And cunning takers of virginities
Caper from bed to bed, but not because
The flesh is pricked to infidelities.

The body is content with homely fare;
It is the avid, curious mind that craves
New pungent sauce and strips the larder bare,
The palate and not hunger that enslaves.

203

Don Juan never was a sensualist:
Scheming fresh triumphs, artful, wary, tense,
He took no pleasure in the breasts he kissed
But gorged his ravenous mind and starved each sense.

An itching, tainted intellectual pride
Goads the salt lecher till he has to know
Whether all women's eyes grow bright and wide,
All wives and whores and virgins shudder so.

Hunters of women burn to show their skill,
Yet when the panting quarry has been caught
Mere force of habit drives them to the kill:
The soft flesh is less savoury than their sport.

Edna St Vincent Millay

I, being born a woman and distressed
By all the needs and notions of my kind,
Am urged by your propinquity to find
Your person fair, and feel a certain zest
To bear your body's weight upon my breast:
So subtly is the fume of life designed,
To clarify the pulse and cloud the mind,
And leave me once again undone, possessed.
Think not for this, however, the poor treason
Of my stout blood against my staggering brain,
I shall remember you with love, or season
My scorn with pity, – let me make it plain:
I find this frenzy insufficient reason
For conversation when we meet again.

Robert Henryson

ROBENE AND MAKYNE

Robene sat on gud grene hill
Kepand a flok of fe;
Mirry Makyne said him till:
'Robene, thow rew on me!
I haif the luvit lowd and still
Thir yeiris two or thre;
My dule in dern bot gif thow dill,
Dowtless but dreid I de.'

Robene ansuerit: 'Be the Rude,
Nathing of lufe I knaw,
Bot keipis my scheip under yone wude —
Lo quhair thay raik on raw!
Quhat hes marrit the in thy mude,
Makyne, to me thow schaw:
Or quhat is lufe, or to be lude?
Fane wald I leir that law.'

'At luvis lair gife thow will leir,
Tak thair ane ABC:
Be heynd, courtas and fair of feir,
Wyse, hardy and fre;
So that no denger do the deir,
Quhat dule in dern thow dre,
Preiss the with pane at all poweir —
Be patient and previe.'

Robene anserit hir agane:
'I wait nocht quhat is luve,
Bot I haif mervell in certane
Quhat makis the this wanrufe;
The weddir is fair and I am fane,
My scheip gois haill aboif;
And we wald play us in this plane
Thay wald us bayth reproif.'

'Robene, tak tent unto my taill,
And wirk all as I reid,
And thow sall haif my hairt all haill,
Eik and my madinheid:
Sen God sendis bute for baill
And for murnyng remeid,
I dern with the bot gif I daill,
Dowtles I am bot deid.'

'Makyne, tomorne this ilka tyde,
And ye will meit me heir,
Peraventure my scheip ma gang besyd
Quhill we haif liggit full neir –
Bot mawgre haif I and I byd,
Fra thay begin to steir;
Quhat lyis on hairt I will nocht hyd;
Makyn, than mak gud cheir.'

'Robene, thow reivis me roif and rest –
I luve bot the allone.'
'Makyne, adew; the sone gois west,
The day is neir-hand gone.'
'Robene, in dule I am so drest
That lufe wil be my bone.'
'Ga lufe, Makyne, quhairever thow list,
For lemman I lue none.'

'Robene, I stand in sic a styll;
I sicht – and that full sair.'
'Makyne, I haif bene heir this quhyle;
At hame God gif I wair!'
'My huny Robene, talk ane quhill,
Gif thow will do na mair.'
'Makyne, stum uthir man begyle,
For hamewart I will fair.'

Robene on his wayis went
Als licht as leif of tre;
Mawkin murnit in hir intent
And trowd him nevir to se.
Robene brayd attour the bent;
Than Mawkyne cryit on hie:
'Now ma thow sing, for I am schent!
Quhat alis lufe at me?'

Mawkyne went hame withowttin faill;
Full wery eftir cowth weip:
Than Robene in a ful fair daill
Assemblit all his scheip.
Be that, sum pairte of Mawkynis aill
Outthrow his hairt cowd creip;
He fallowit fast thair till assaill,
And till hir tuke gude keip.

'Abyd, abyd, thow fair Makyne!
A word for ony thing!
For all my luve it sal be thyne,
Withowttin depairting.
All haill thy harte for till haif myne
Is all my cuvating;
My scheip tomorne quhill houris nyne
Will neid of no keiping.'

'Robene, thow hes hard soung and say
In gestis and storeis auld,
The man that will nocht quhen he may
Sall haif nocht quhen he wald.
I pray to Jesu every day
Mot eik thair cairis cauld
That first preiss with the to play
Be firth, forrest or fawld.'

'Makyne, the nicht is soft and dry,
The wedder is warme and fair,
And the grene woid rycht neir us by
To walk attour allquhair;
Thair ma na janglour us espy,
That is to lufe contrair;
Thairin, Makyne, bath ye and I
Unsene we ma repair.'

'Robene, that warld is all away
And quyt brocht till ane end,
And nevir agane thairto perfay,
Sall it be as thow wend:
For of my pane thow maid it play,
And all in vane I spend:
And thow hes done, sa sall I say:
Murne on! I think to mend.'

'Mawkyne, the howp of all my heill,
My hairt on the is sett,
And evirmair to the be leill,
Quhill I may leif but lett;
Nevir to faill – as utheris feill –
Quhat grace that evir I gett.'
'Robene, with the I will nocht deill;
Adew! For thus we mett.'

Malkyne went hame blyth annewche
Attour the holttis hair:
Robene murnit, and Malkyne lewche,
Scho sang, he sichit sair –
And so left him bayth wo and wrewche,
In dolour and in cair,
Kepand his hird under a huche,
Amangis the holtis hair.

kepand keeping
fe sheep, cattle
him till to him
dule in dern sorrow in secret
dill soothe
but dreid I de I shall certainly die
raik on raw range in row
marrit perplexed
mude mind
lude loved
leir learn
lair lore
heynd gentle
feir demeanour
denger disdain
deir harm
dre endure
preiss endeavour
wanrufe restless
fane glad
haill healthy, whole
aboif up yonder
and if
tak tent give heed
reid advise
bute for baill remedy for hurt
bot gif but if, unless
mawgre haif I and I am uneasy if
reivis robbest
roif quiet

drest beset
bone bane
lemman mistress
styll plight
sicht sigh
intent mind
brayd strode
bent coarse grass
schent destroyed
alis ails
cowth did
be that by the time that
till to
tuke gude keip centred his
   thoughts, paid attention
hard heard
gestis romances
mot eik may add to
cairis sorrows
be by
janglour talebearer
wend weened
howp hope
leill true
but lett without hindrance
annewche enough
holttis hair grey woodlands
lewche laughed
wrewche peevish
huche cliff

George Wither

A LOVER'S RESOLUTION

Shall I, wasting in despair,
Die because a woman's fair?
Or make pale my cheeks with care
'Cause another's rosy are?
Be she fairer than the day,
Or the flowery meads in May,
  If she be not so to me,
  What care I how fair she be?

Should my heart be grieved or pined
'Cause I see a woman kind?
Or a well disposed nature
Joinèd with a lovely feature?
Be she meeker, kinder, than
Turtle-dove or pelican,
  If she be not so to me,
  What care I how kind she be?

Shall a woman's virtues move
Me to perish for her love?
Or her well-deserving known
Make me quite forget my own?
Be she with that goodness blessed
Which may gain her name of Best,
  If she be not such to me,
  What care I how good she be?

'Cause her fortune seems too high,
Shall I play the fool and die?
Those that bear a noble mind,
Where they want of riches find,

Think what with them they would do
That without them dare to woo;
    And unless that mind I see,
    What care I though great she be?

Great, or good, or kind, or fair,
I will ne'er the more despair;
If she love me, this believe,
I will die ere she shall grieve;
If she slight me when I woo,
I can scorn and let her go;
    For if she be not for me,
    What care I for whom she be?

A. E. Housman

Oh, when I was in love with you,
    Then I was clean and brave,
And miles around the wonder grew
    How well did I behave.

And now the fancy passes by,
    And nothing will remain,
And miles around they'll say that I
    Am quite myself again.

Bhartṛhari

In former days we'd both agree
That you were me, and I was you.
What has now happened to us two,
That you are you, and I am me?

Translated from the Sanskrit by
John Brough

Robert Graves

THE THIEVES

Lovers in the act dispense
With such meum-tuum sense
As might warningly reveal
What they must not pick or steal,
And their nostrum is to say:
'I and you are both away.'

After, when they disentwine
You from me and yours from mine,
Neither can be certain who
Was that I whose mine was you.
To the act again they go
More completely not to know.

Theft is theft and raid is raid
Though reciprocally made.
Lovers, the conclusion is
Doubled sighs and jealousies
In a single heart that grieves
For lost honour among thieves.

Abraham Cowley

THE WELCOME

Go, let the fatted calf be killed;
  My Prodigal's come home at last;
With noble resolutions filled,
  And filled with sorrow for the past.
  No more will burn with love or wine:
But quite has left his women and his swine.

Welcome, ah welcome my poor Heart;
    Welcome; I little thought, I'll swear,
('Tis now so long since we did part)
    Ever again to see thee here:
    Dear Wanderer, since from me you fled,
How often have I heard that thou wert dead!

Hast thou not found each woman's breast
    (The lands where thou hast travelled)
Either by savages possessed,
    Or wild, and uninhabited?
    What joy could'st take, or what repose
In countries so uncivilized as those?

Lust, the scorching Dog-star, here
    Rages with immoderate heat;
Whilst Pride the rugged Northern Bear,
    In others makes the cold too great.
    And where these are temperate known,
The soil's all barren sand, or rocky stone.

When once or twice you chanced to view
    A rich, well-governed heart,
Like China, it admitted you
    But to the frontier-part.
    From Paradise shut for evermore,
What good is't that an angel kept the door?

Well fare the pride, and the disdain,
    And vanities with beauty joined,
I ne'er had seen this Heart again,
    If any fair one had been kind:
    My dove, but once let loose, I doubt
Would ne'er return, had not the flood been out.

Sir John Suckling

Out upon it, I have loved
   Three whole days together;
And am like to love three more,
   If it hold fair weather.

Time shall moult away his wings
   Ere he shall discover
In the whole wide world again
   Such a constant lover.

But a pox upon't, no praise
   There is due at all to me:
Love with me had made no stays,
   Had it any been but she.

Had it any been but she
   And that very very face,
There had been at least ere this
   A dozen dozen in her place.

John Wilmot, Earl of Rochester

LOVE AND LIFE

All my past life is mine no more;
   The flying hours are gone,
Like transitory dreams given o'er
Whose images are kept in store
   By memory alone.

Whatever is to come is not:
　　How can it then be mine?
The present moment's all my lot,
And that, as fast as it is got,
　　Phyllis, is wholly thine.

Then talk not of inconstancy,
　　False hearts, and broken vows;
If I, by miracle, can be
This livelong minute true to thee,
　　'Tis all that heaven allows.

Richard Lovelace

THE SCRUTINY

Why should you swear I am forsworn,
　　Since thine I vowed to be?
Lady it is already morn,
　　And 'twas last night I swore to thee
That fond impossibility.

Have I not loved thee much and long,
　　A tedious twelve hours' space?
I must all other Beauties wrong,
　　And rob thee of a new embrace;
Could I still dote upon thy face.

Not, but all joy in thy brown hair,
　　By others may be found;
But I must search the black and fair
　　Like skilful mineralists that sound
For treasure in un-plowed-up ground.

Then, if when I have loved my round,
   Thou provest the pleasant she;
With spoils of meaner Beauties crowned,
   I laden will return to thee,
Ev'n sated with variety.

Martial

Lycóris darling, once I burned for you,
Today Glýcera heats me like a stew:
She's what you were then but are not now —
A change of name requires no change of vow.

Translated from the Latin by
Peter Porter

John Donne

THE INDIFFERENT

I can love both fair and brown,
Her whom abundance melts, and her whom want betrays,
Her who loves loneness best, and her who masks and plays,
   Her whom the country formed, and whom the town,
   Her who believes, and her who tries,
   Her who still weeps with spongy eyes,
And her who is dry cork, and never cries;
I can love her, and her, and you and you,
I can love any, so she be not true.

   Will no other vice content you?
Will it not serve your turn to do, as did your mothers?
Or have you old vices spent, and now would find out
  others?
   Or doth a fear, that men are true, torment you?

Oh we are not, be not you so,
    Let me, and do you, twenty know.
Rob me, but bind me not, and let me go.
Must I, who came to travail thorough you,
Grow your fixed subject, because you are true?

        Venus heard me sigh this song,
And by Love's sweetest part, variety, she swore,
She heard not this till now; and and't should be so no
    more.
        She went, examined, and returned ere long,
            And said, alas, Some two or three
            Poor heretics in love there be,
        Which think to stablish dangerous constancy.
        But I have told them, since you will be true,
        You shall be true to them, who are false to you.

D. H. Lawrence

INTIMATES

Don't you care for my love? she said bitterly.

I handed her the mirror, and said:
Please address these questions to the proper person!
Please make all requests to head-quarters!
In all matters of emotional importance
please approach the supreme authority direct! –
So I handed her the mirror.

And she would have broken it over my head,
but she caught sight of her own reflection
and that held her spellbound for two seconds
while I fled.

Bhartṛhari

She who is always in my thoughts prefers
Another man, and does not think of me.
Yet he seeks for another's love, not hers;
And some poor girl is grieving for my sake.
    Why then, the devil take
Both her and him; and love; and her; and me.

Translated from the Sanskrit by
John Brough

Walter Savage Landor

You smiled, you spoke, and I believed,
By every word and smile deceived.
Another man would hope no more;
Nor hope I what I hoped before:
But let not this last wish be vain;
Deceive, deceive me once again!

Richard Weber

ELIZABETH IN ITALY

'Suddenly she slapped me, hard across the face.
I implored, but she declined to have any further
Social or sexual (so she put it) intercourse with me.
Neither would she give me either a personal picture
Or a lock of her most beautiful hair.
Indeed, she demanded, her exquisite voice
Quite hard, the return of her handkerchief
And any other things (I murmured, "mementoes,"
But she repeated "things") I might have stolen
From her in my privileged position as her servant.
God only knew what had made her ask me
Fetch her the bathrobe that terrible night.
("That beautiful night," I recollected aloud.)
Did I believe our positions were reversed?
(I whitened at the accusation.) Well, then,
She wished to make clear now and for so long
As the relationship ("Madam!" cried I) lasted,
That it could only do so if I went to bed first,
Where she would come at her pleasure.
I could make no clearer sign of my heartfelt
Gratitude and infinite relief at these words
Than by the impassioned and repeated kissing,
There and then, of her magnificent left breast
Which had come out of hiding towards the end
Of her peroration. Whereupon she slapped me again.'

John Wilmot, Earl of Rochester

A SONG

Absent from thee, I languish still;
    Then ask me not, when I return?
The straying fool 'twill plainly kill
    To wish all day, all night to mourn.

Dear! from thine arms then let me fly,
    That my fantastic mind may prove
The torments it deserves to try
    That tears my fixed heart from my love.

When, wearied with a world of woe,
    To thy safe bosom I retire
Where love and peace and truth does flow,
    May I contented there expire,

Lest, once more wandering from that heaven,
    I fall on some base heart unblessed,
Faithless to thee, false, unforgiven,
    And lose my everlasting rest.

Robert Graves

A SLICE OF WEDDING CAKE

Why have such scores of lovely, gifted girls
    Married impossible men?
Simple self-sacrifice may be ruled out,
    And missionary endeavour, nine times out of ten.

Repeat 'impossible men': not merely rustic,
    Foul-tempered or depraved
(Dramatic foils chosen to show the world
    How well women behave, and always have behaved).

Impossible men: idle, illiterate,
    Self-pitying, dirty, sly,
For whose appearance even in City parks
    Excuses must be made to casual passers-by.

Has God's supply of tolerable husbands
    Fallen, in fact, so low?
Or do I always over-value woman
    At the expense of man?
               Do I?
                    It might be so.

SEPARATIONS

Anon

SEVENTEENTH CENTURY

Walking in a meadow green,
  fair flowers for to gather,
where primrose ranks did stand on banks
  to welcome comers thither,
I heard a voice which made a noise,
  which caused me to attend it,
I heard a lass say to a lad,
  'Once more, & none can mend it.'

They lay so close together,
  they made me much to wonder;
I know not which was wether,
  until I saw her under.
Then off her came, & blushed for shame
  so soon that he had ended;
yet still she lies, & to him cries,
  'Once more, & none can mend it.'

His looks were dull & very sad,
  his courage she had tamed;
she bade him play the lusty lad
  or else he quite was shamed;
'then stiffly thrust, he hit me just,
  fear not, but freely spend it,
& play about at in & out;
  once more, & none can mend it.'

And then he thought to venter her,
  thinking the fit was on him;
but when he came to enter her,
  the point turned back upon him.

225

Yet she said, 'stay! go not away
    although the point he bended!
but toot again, & hit the vane!
    once more, & none can mend it.'

Then in her armes she did him fold,
    & oftentimes she kissed him,
yet still his courage was but cold
    for all the good she wished him;
yet with her hand she made it stand
    so stiff she could not bend it,
& then anon she cries 'come on
    once more, & none can mend it!'

'Adieu, adieu, sweet heart,' quoth he,
    'for in faith I must be gone.'
'Nay, then you do me wrong,' quoth she,
    'to leave me thus alone.'
Away he went when all was spent,
    whereat she was offended;
Like a Trojan true she made a vow
    she would have one should mend it.

ventor penetrate

Thom Gunn

CARNAL KNOWLEDGE

Even in bed I pose: desire may grow
More circumstantial and less circumspect
Each night, but an acute girl would suspect
My thoughts might not be, like my body, bare.
I wonder if you know, or, knowing care?
You know I know you know I know you know.

I am not what I seem, believe me, so
For the magnanimous pagan I pretend
Substitute a forked creature as your friend.
When darkness lies – without a roll or stir –
Flaccid, you want a competent poseur
Whose seeming is the only thing to know.

I prod you, you react. Thus to and fro
We turn, to see ourselves perform the same
Comical act inside the tragic game.
Or is it perhaps simpler: could it be
A mere tear-jerker void of honesty
In which there are no motives left to know?

Lie back. Within a minute I will stow
Your greedy mouth, but will not yet to grips.
'There is a space between the breast and lips.'
Also a space between the thighs and head,
So great, we might as well not be in bed:
For we learn nothing here we did not know.

I hardly hoped for happy thoughts, although
In a most happy sleeping time I dreamt
We did not hold each other in contempt.
Then lifting from my lids night's penny weights
I saw that lack of love contaminates.
You know I know you know I know you know.

Abandon me to stammering, and go;
If you have tears, prepare to cry elsewhere –
I know of no emotion we can share.
Your intellectual protests are a bore,
And even now I pose, so now go, for
I know you know.

Anon

She lay all naked in her bed,
    And I myself lay by;
No veil but curtains about her spread,
    No covering but I:
Her head upon her shoulders seeks
    To hang in careless wise,
And full of blushes was her cheeks,
    And of wishes were her eyes.

Her blood still fresh into her face,
    As on a message came,
To say that in another place
    It meant another game;
Her cherry lip moist, plump, and fair,
    Millions of kisses crown,
Which ripe and uncropped dangled there,
    And weigh the branches down.

Her breasts, that welled so plump and high
    Bred pleasant pain in me,
For all the world I do defy
    The like felicity;
Her thighs and belly, soft and fair,
    To me were only shown:
To have seen such meat, and not to have eat,
    Would have angered any stone.

Her knees lay upward gently bent,
    And all lay hollow under,
As if on easy terms, they meant
    To fall unforced asunder;

Just so the Cyprian Queen did lie,
    Expecting in her bower;
When too long stay had kept the boy
    Beyond his promised hour.

'Dull clown,' quoth she, 'why dost delay
    Such proffered bliss to take?
Canst thou find out no other way
    Similitudes to make?'
Mad with delight I thundering
    Throw my arms about her,
But pox upon't 'twas but a dream.
    And so I lay without her.

Anon

AUBADE

SIXTEENTH CENTURY

Stay, O sweet, and do not rise,
The light that shines comes from thine eyes;
The day breaks not, it is my heart,
Because that you and I must part.
    Stay, or else my joys will die,
    And perish in their infancy.

John Donne

SONG

Sweetest love, I do not go
    For weariness of thee,
Nor in hope the world can show
    A fitter love for me;

But since that I
Must die at last, 'tis best
To use myself in jest
   Thus by fained deaths to die.

Yesternight the sun went hence,
   And yet is here today,
He hath no desire nor sense,
   Nor half so short a way:
    Then fear not me,
But believe that I shall make
Speedier journeys, since I take
   More wings and spurs than he.

O how feeble is man's power,
   That if good fortune fall,
Cannot add another hour,
   Nor a lost hour recall!
    But come bad chance,
And we join to it our strength,
And we teach it art and length,
   Itself o'er us to advance.

When thou sigh'st, thou sigh'st not wind,
   But sigh'st my soul away,
When thou weep'st, unkindly kind,
   My life's blood doth decay.
    It cannot be
That thou lov'st me, as thou say'st,
If in thine my life thou waste,
   Thou art the best of me.

Let not thy divining heart
   Forethink me any ill,
Destiny may take thy part,
   And may thy fears fulfil;

But think that we
Are but turned aside to sleep;
They who one another keep
Alive, ne'er parted be.

Robert Burns

A RED RED ROSE

O my Luve's like a red, red rose,
That's newly sprung in June;
O my Luve's like the melodie
That's sweetly play'd in tune. –

As fair art thou, my bonie lass,
So deep in luve am I;
And I will love thee still, my Dear,
Till a' the seas gang dry. –

Till a' the seas gang dry, my Dear,
And the rocks melt wi' the sun:
I will love thee still, my Dear,
While the sands o' life shall run. –

And fare thee weel, my only Luve!
And fare thee weel, a while!
And I will come again, my Luve,
Tho' it were ten thousand mile!

Hart Crane

CARRIER LETTER

My hands have not touched water since your hands, —
No; — nor my lips freed laughter since 'farewell'.
And with the day, distance again expands
Between us, voiceless as an uncoiled shell.

Yet, — much follows, much endures ... Trust birds alone:
A dove's wings clung about my heart last night
With surging gentleness; and the blue stone
Set in the tryst-ring has but worn more bright.

E. E. Cummings

it may not always be so; and i say
that if your lips, which i have loved, should touch
another's, and your dear strong fingers clutch
his heart, as mine in time not far away;
if on another's face your sweet hair lay
in such a silence as i know, or such
great writhing words as, uttering overmuch,
stand helplessly before the spirit at bay;

if this should be, i say if this should be —
you of my heart, send me a little word;
that i may go unto him, and take his hands,
saying, Accept all happiness from me.
Then shall i turn my face, and hear one bird
sing terribly afar in the lost lands.

Alun Lewis

POSTSCRIPT: FOR GWENO

If I should go away,
Beloved, do not say
'He has forgotten me'.
For you abide,
A singing rib within my dreaming side;
You always stay.
And in the mad tormented valley
Where blood and hunger rally
And Death the wild beast is uncaught, untamed,
Our soul withstands the terror
And has its quiet honour
Among the glittering stars your voices named.

W. H. Auden

Dear, though the night is gone,
Its dream still haunts today,
That brought us to a room
Cavernous, lofty as
A railway terminus,
And crowded in that gloom
Were beds, and we in one
In a far corner lay.

Our whisper woke no clocks,
We kissed and I was glad
At everything you did,

Indifferent to those
Who sat with hostile eyes
In pairs on every bed,
Arms round each other's neck,
Inert and vaguely sad.

O but what worm of guilt
Or what malignant doubt
Am I the victim of,
That you then, unabashed,
Did what I never wished,
Confessed another love;
And I, submissive, felt
Unwanted and went out?

Robert Browning

THE LAST RIDE TOGETHER

I said – Then, dearest, since 'tis so,
Since now at length my fate I know,
Since nothing all my love avails,
Since all, my life seemed meant for, fails,
    Since this was written and needs must be –
My whole heart rises up to bless
Your name in pride and thankfulness!
Take back the hope you gave, I claim
Only a memory of the same,
– And this beside, if you will not blame,
    Your leave for one more last ride with me.

My mistress bent that brow of hers;
Those deep dark eyes where pride demurs
When pity would be softening through,
Fixed me a breathing-while or two
    With life or death in the balance: right!
The blood replenished me again;
My last thought was at least not vain:
I and my mistress, side by side
Shall be together, breathe and ride,
So, one day more am I deified.
    Who knows but the world may end tonight?

Hush! if you saw some western cloud
All billowy-bosomed, over-bowed
By many benedictions – sun's
And moon's and evening-star's at once –
    And so, you, looking and loving best,
Conscious grew, your passion drew
Cloud, sunset, moonrise, star-shine too,
Down on you, near and yet more near,
Till flesh must fade for heaven was here! –
Thus leant she and lingered – joy and fear!
    Thus lay she a moment on my breast.

Then we began to ride. My soul
Smoothed itself out, a long-cramped scroll
Freshening and fluttering in the wind.
Past hopes already lay behind.
    What need to strive with a life awry?
Had I said that, had I done this,
So might I gain, so might I miss.
Might she have loved me? just as well
She might have hated, who can tell!
Where had I been now if the worst befell?
    And here we are riding, she and I.

Fail I alone, in words and deeds?
Why, all men strive and who succeeds?
We rode; it seemed my spirit flew,
Saw other regions, cities new,
 As the world rushed by on either side.
I thought, – All labour, yet no less
Bear up beneath their unsuccess.
Look at the end of work, contrast
The petty done, the undone vast,
This present of theirs with the hopeful past!
 I hoped she would love me; here we ride.

What hand and brain went ever paired?
What heart alike conceived and dared?
What act proved all its thought had been?
What will but felt the fleshly screen?
 We ride and I see her bosom heave.
There's many a crown for who can reach.
Ten lines, a statesman's life in each!
The flag stuck on a heap of bones,
A soldier's doing! what atones?
They scratch his name on the Abbey-stones.
 My riding is better, by their leave.

What does it all mean, poet? Well,
Your brains beat into rhythm, you tell
What we felt only; you expressed
You hold things beautiful the best,
 And pace them in rhyme so, side by side.
'Tis something, nay 'tis much: but then,
Have you yourself what's best for men?
Are you – poor, sick, old ere your time –
Nearer one whit your own sublime
Than we who never have turned a rhyme?
 Sing, riding's a joy! For me, I ride.

And you, great sculptor – so, you gave
A score of years to Art, her slave,
And that's your Venus, whence we turn
To yonder girl that fords the burn!
   You acquiesce, and shall I repine?
What, man of music, you grown grey
With notes and nothing else to say,
Is this your sole praise from a friend,
'Greatly his opera's strains intend,
'But in music we know how fashions end!'
   I gave my youth; but we ride, in fine.

Who knows what's fit for us? Had fate
Proposed bliss here should sublimate
My being – had I signed the bond –
Still one must lead some life beyond,
   Have a bliss to die with, dim-descried.
This foot once planted on the goal,
This glory-garland round my soul,
Could I descry such? Try and test!
I sink back shuddering from the quest.
Earth being so good, would heaven seem best?
   Now, heaven and she are beyond this ride.

And yet – she has not spoke so long!
What if heaven be that, fair and strong
At life's best, with our eyes upturned
Whither life's flower is first discerned,
   We, fixed so, ever should so abide?
What if we still ride on, we two
With life for ever old yet new,
Changed not in kind but in degree
The instant made eternity, –
And heaven just prove that I and she
   Ride, ride together, for ever ride?

Robert Browning

THE LOST MISTRESS

All's over, then: does truth sound bitter
   As one at first believes?
Hark, 'tis the sparrows' good-night twitter
   About your cottage eaves!

And the leaf-buds on the vine are woolly,
   I noticed that, today;
One day more bursts them open fully
   – You know the red turns grey.

Tomorrow we meet the same then, dearest?
   May I take your hand in mine?
Mere friends are we, – well, friends the merest
   Keep much that I resign:

For each glance of the eye so bright and black,
   Though I keep with heart's endeavour, –
Your voice, when you wish the snowdrops back,
   Though it stay in my soul for ever! –

Yet I will but say what mere friends say,
   Or only a thought stronger;
I will hold your hand but as long as all may,
   Or so very little longer!

Michael Drayton

Since there's no help, come let us kiss and part —
Nay, I have done, you get no more of me;
And I am glad, yea, glad with all my heart,
That thus so cleanly I myself can free.
Shake hands for ever, cancel all our vows,
And when we meet at any time again,
Be it not seen in either of our brows
That we one jot of former love retain.
Now at the last gasp of Love's latest breath,
When, his pulse failing, Passion speechless lies,
When Faith is kneeling by his bed of death,
And Innocence is closing up his eyes,
   — Now if thou would'st, when all have given him over,
   From death to life thou might'st him yet recover.

Ernest Dowson

A VALEDICTION

If we must part,
   Then let it be like this;
Not heart on heart,
   Nor with the useless anguish of a kiss;
But touch mine hand and say;
'Until tomorrow or some other day,
   If we must part.'

Words are so weak
   When love hath been so strong:
Let silence speak:

' Life is a little while, and love is long;
A time to sow and reap,
And after harvest a long time to sleep,
*   But words are weak.'*

Coventry Patmore

A FAREWELL

With all my will, but much against my heart,
We two now part.
My Very Dear,
Our solace is, the sad road lies so clear.
It needs no art,
With faint, averted feet
And many a tear,
In our opposed paths to persevere.
Go thou to East, I West.
We will not say
There's any hope, it is so far away.
But, O, my Best,
When the one darling of our widowhead,
The nursling Grief,
Is dead,
And no dews blur our eyes
To see the peach-bloom come in evening skies,
Perchance we may,
Where now this night is day,
And even through faith of still averted feet,
Making full circle of our banishment,
Amazed meet;
The bitter journey to the bourne so sweet
Seasoning the termless feast of our content
With tears of recognition never dry.

Alun Lewis

GOODBYE

So we must say Goodbye, my darling,
And go, as lovers go, for ever;
Tonight remains, to pack and fix on labels
And make an end of lying down together.

I put a final shilling in the gas,
And watch you slip your dress below your knees
And lie so still I hear your rustling comb
Modulate the autumn in the trees.

And all the countless things I shall remember
Lay mummy-cloths of silence round my head;
I fill the carafe with a drink of water;
You say 'We paid a guinea for this bed,'

And then, 'We'll leave some gas, a little warmth
For the next resident, and these dry flowers,'
And turn your face away, afraid to speak
The big word, that Eternity is ours.

Your kisses close my eyes and yet you stare
As though God struck a child with nameless fears;
Perhaps the water glitters and discloses
Time's chalice and its limpid useless tears.

Everything we renounce except our selves;
Selfishness is the last of all to go;
Our sighs are exhalations of the earth,
Our footprints leave a track across the snow.

We made the universe to be our home,
Our nostrils took the wind to be our breath,
Our hearts are massive towers of delight,
We stride across the seven seas of death.

Yet when all's done you'll keep the emerald
I placed upon your finger in the street;
And I will keep the patches that you sewed
On my old battledress tonight, my sweet.

John Donne

ON HIS MISTRESS

By our first strange and fatal interview,
By all desires which thereof did ensue,
By our long starving hopes, by that remorse
Which my words' masculine persuasive force
Begot in thee, and by the memory
Of hurts which spies and rivals threatened me,
I calmly beg; but by thy parents' wrath,
By all pains which want and divorcement hath,
I conjure thee; and all those oaths which I
And thou have sworn, to seal joint constancy,
Here I unswear, and overswear them thus:
Thou shalt not love by means so dangerous.
Temper, O fair Love, love's impetuous rage,
Be my true mistress still, not my feigned page.
I'll go, and, by thy kind leave, leave behind
Thee, only worthy to nurse in my mind
Thirst to come back; O, if thou die before,
From other lands my soul towards thee shall soar.

Thy (else almighty) beauty cannot move
Rage from the seas, nor thy love teach them love,
Nor tame wild Boreas' harshness: thou hast read
How roughly he in pieces shiverèd
Fair Orithea, whom he swore he loved.
Fall ill or good, 'tis madness to have proved
Dangers unurged; feed on this flattery,
That absent lovers one in the other be.
Dissemble nothing, not a boy, nor change
Thy body's habit, nor mind's; be not strange
To thyself only; all will spy in thy face
A blushing womanly discovering grace.
Richly clothed apes are called apes, and as soon
Eclipsed as bright, we call the moon the moon.
Men of France, changeable chameleons,
Spittles of diseases, shops of fashions,
Love's fuellers, and the rightest company
Of players, which upon the world's stage be,
Will quickly know thee, and know thee; and alas,
The indifferent Italian, as we pass
His warm land, well content to think thee page,
Will haunt thee, with such lust and hideous rage
As Lot's fair guests were vexed: but none of these,
Nor spongy hydroptic Dutch, shall thee displease,
If thou stay here. O stay here, for, for thee
England is only a worthy gallery,
To walk in expectation, till from thence
Our great King call thee into his presence.
When I am gone, dream me some happiness,
Nor let thy looks our long-hid love confess,
Nor praise, nor dispraise me, bless, nor curse
Openly love's force; nor in bed fright thy nurse
With midnight's startings, crying out, 'Oh, Oh,
Nurse, Oh, my love is slain; I saw him go

O'er the white Alps, alone; I saw him, I,
Assailed, fight, taken, stabbed, bleed, fall, and die.'
Augur me better chance, except dread Jove
Think it enough for me to have had thy love.

spittles hospitals

John Gay

SWEET WILLIAM'S FAREWELL TO BLACK-EYED SUSAN

All in the Downs the fleet was moored,
  The streamers waving in the wind,
When black-eyed Susan came aboard,
    'Oh! where shall I my true love find?
Tell me, ye jovial sailors, tell me true,
If my sweet William sails among the crew.'

  William, who high upon the yard,
    Rocked with the billow to and fro,
Soon as her well-known voice he heard,
    He sighed, and cast his eyes below:
The cord slides swiftly through his glowing hands
And, quick as lightning, on the deck he stands.

  So the sweet lark, high-poised in air,
    Shuts close his pinions to his breast,
If, chance, his mate's shrill call he hear
    And drops at once into her nest.
The noblest captain in the British fleet,
Might envy William's lip those kisses sweet.

'O Susan, Susan, lovely dear,
    My vows shall ever true remain;
Let me kiss off that falling tear,
    We only part to meet again.
Change, as ye list, ye winds; my heart shall be
The faithful compass that still points to thee.

Believe not what the landsmen say,
    Who tempt with doubts thy constant mind:
They'll tell thee, sailors, when away,
    In every port a mistress find.
Yes, yes, believe them when they tell thee so,
For thou art present whereso'er I go.

If to far India's coast we sail,
    Thy eyes are seen in diamonds bright,
Thy breath is Afric's spicy gale,
    Thy skin is ivory, so white.
Thus every beauteous object that I view,
Wakes in my soul some charm of lovely Sue.

Though battle call me from thy arms,
    Let not my pretty Susan mourn;
Though cannons roar, yet safe from harms,
    William shall to his dear return.
Love turns aside the balls that round me fly,
Lest precious tears should drop from Susan's eye.'

The boatswain gave the dreadful word,
    The sails their swelling bosom spread,
No longer must she stay aboard:
    They kissed, she sighed, he hung his head.
Her lessening boat unwilling rows to land:
'Adieu,' she cries, and waved her lily hand.

Robert Burns

SONG

Ae fond kiss, and then we sever;
Ae fareweel, and then for ever!
Deep in heart-wrung tears I'll pledge thee,
Warring sighs and groans I'll wage thee. –

Who shall say that Fortune grieves him,
While the star of hope she leaves him:
Me, nae chearful twinkle lights me;
Dark despair around benights me. –

I'll ne'er blame my partial fancy,
Naething could resist my Nancy:
But to see her, was to love her;
Love but her, and love for ever. –

Had we never lov'd sae kindly,
Had we never lov'd sae blindly!
Never met – or never parted,
We had ne'er been broken-hearted. –

Fare-thee-weel, thou first and fairest!
Fare-thee-weel, thou best and dearest!
Thine be ilka joy and treasure,
Peace, Enjoyment, Love and Pleasure! –

Ae fond kiss, and then we sever!
Ae fareweel, Alas, for ever!
Deep in heart-wrung tears I'll pledge thee,
Warring sighs and groans I'll wage thee. –

Emily Dickinson

My life closed twice before its close —
It yet remains to see
If Immortality unveil
A third event to me

So huge, so hopeless to conceive
As these that twice befell.
Parting is all we know of heaven,
And all we need of hell.

Edward Thomas

LIKE THE TOUCH OF RAIN

Like the touch of rain she was
On a man's flesh and hair and eyes
When the joy of walking thus
Has taken him by surprise:

With the love of the storm he burns,
He sings, he laughs, well I know how,
But forgets when he returns
As I shall not forget her 'Go now'.

Those two words shut a door
Between me and the blessed rain
That was never shut before
And will not open again.

Harold Monro

THE TERRIBLE DOOR

Too long outside your door I have shivered.
You open it? I will not stay.
I'm haunted by your ashen beauty.
Take back your hand. I have gone away.

Don't talk, but move to that near corner.
I loathe the long cold shadow here.
We will stand a moment in the lamplight,
Until I watch you hard and near.

Happy release! Good-bye for ever!
Here at the corner we say good-bye.
But if you want me, if you do need me,
Who waits, at the terrible door, but I?

Thomas Hardy

IN THE VAULTED WAY

In the vaulted way, where the passage turned
To the shadowy corner that none could see,
You paused for our parting, – plaintively:
Though overnight had come words that burned
My fond frail happiness out of me.

And then I kissed you, – despite my thought
That our spell must end when reflection came
On what you had deemed me, whose one long aim
Had been to serve you; that what I sought
Lay not in a heart that could breathe such blame.

But yet I kissed you: whereon you again
As of old kissed me. Why, why was it so?
Do you cleave to me after that light-tongued blow?
If you scorned me at eventide, how love then?
The thing is dark, Dear. I do not know.

Anna Akhmatova

I wrung my hands under my dark veil . . .
'Why are you pale, what makes you reckless?'
– Because I have made my loved one drunk
with an astringent sadness.

I'll never forget. He went out, reeling;
his mouth was twisted, desolate . . .
I ran downstairs, not touching the banisters,
and followed him as far as the gate.

And shouted, choking: 'I meant it all
in fun. Don't leave me, or I'll die of pain.'
He smiled at me – oh so calmly, terribly –
and said: 'Why don't you get out of the rain?'

Translated from the Russian by
Max Hayward and Stanley Kunitz

Brian Patten

PARTY PIECE

He said:

'Let's stay here
Now this place has emptied
And make gentle pornography with one another,
While the partygoers go out
And the dawn creeps in,
Like a stranger.

Let us not hesitate
Over what we know
Or over how cold this place has become,
But lets unclip our minds
And let tumble free
The mad, mangled crocodile of love.'

So they did,
There among the woodbines and guinness stains,
And later he caught a bus and she a train
And all there was between them then
was rain.

Yehuda Amichai

A PITY. WE WERE SUCH A GOOD INVENTION

They amputated
Your thighs off my hips.
As far as I'm concerned
They are all surgeons. All of them.

They dismantled us
Each from the other.
As far as I'm concerned
They are all engineers. All of them.

A pity. We were such a good
And loving invention.
An aeroplane made from a man and wife.
Wings and everything.
We hovered a little above the earth.

We even flew a little.

Translated from the Hebrew by
Assia Gutmann

Lord Byron

When we two parted
In silence and tears,
Half broken-hearted,
To sever for years,
Pale grew thy cheek and cold,
Colder thy kiss;
Truly that hour foretold
Sorrow to this!

The dew of the morning
Sunk chill on my brow;
It felt like the warning
Of what I feel now.
Thy vows are all broken,
And light is thy fame:
I hear thy name spoken
And share in its shame.

They name thee before me,
A knell to mine ear;
A shudder comes o'er me –
Why wert thou so dear?
They know not I knew thee
Who knew thee too well:
Long, long shall I rue thee
Too deeply to tell.

In secret we met:
In silence I grieve
That thy heart could forget,
Thy spirit deceive.
If I should meet thee
After long years,
How should I greet thee? –
With silence and tears.

Alice Meynell

RENOUNCEMENT

I must not think of thee; and, tired yet strong,
I shun the thought that lurks in all delight –
   The thought of thee – and in the blue heaven's height,
And in the sweetest passage of a song.
Oh, just beyond the fairest thoughts that throng
   This breast, the thought of thee waits hidden yet bright;
But it must never, never come in sight;
I must stop short of thee the whole day long.

But when sleep comes to close each difficult day,
   When night gives pause to the long watch I keep,
And all my bonds I needs must loose apart,
Must doff my will as raiment laid away, —
   With the first dream that comes with the first sleep
I run, I run, I am gathered to thy heart.

Alain Chartier

     I turn you out of doors
     tenant desire

     you pay no rent
     I turn you out of doors
     all my best rooms are yours
     the brain and heart

              depart
     I turn you out of doors

     switch off the lights
     throw water on the fire
     I turn you out of doors

     stubborn desire

*Translated from the French by
Edward Lucie-Smith*

Alexander Pope

EPISTLE TO MISS BLOUNT,
ON HER LEAVING THE TOWN,
AFTER THE CORONATION

As some fond virgin, whom her mother's care
Drags from the town to wholesome country air,
Just when she learns to roll a melting eye,
And hear a spark, yet think no danger nigh;
From the dear man unwilling she must sever,
Yet takes one kiss before she parts for ever:
Thus from the world fair Zephalinda flew,
Saw others happy, and with sighs withdrew;
Not that their pleasures caused her discontent,
She sighed not that They stayed, but that She went.
   She went, to plain-work, and to purling brooks,
Old-fashioned halls, dull aunts, and croaking rooks,
She went from Opera, park, assembly, play,
To morning walks, and prayers three hours a day;
To pass her time 'twixt reading and Bohea,
To muse, and spill her solitary tea,
Or o'er cold coffee trifle with the spoon,
Count the slow clock, and dine exact at noon;
Divert her eyes with pictures in the fire,
Hum half a tune, tell stories to the squire;
Up to her godly garret after seven,
There starve and pray, for that's the way to heaven.
   Some Squire, perhaps, you take a delight to rack;
Whose game is Whisk, whose treat a toast in sack,
Who visits with a gun, presents you birds,
Then gives a smacking buss, and cries – No words!
Or with his hound comes hollowing from the stable,
Makes love with nods, and knees beneath a table;

Whose laughs are hearty, tho' his jests are coarse,
And loves you best of all things – but his horse.
   In some fair evening, on your elbow laid,
You dream of triumphs in the rural shade;
In pensive thought recall the fancied scene,
See Coronations rise on every green;
Before you pass th' imaginary sights
Of Lords, and Earls, and Dukes, and gartered Knights;
While the spread fan o'ershades your closing eyes;
Then give one flirt, and all the vision flies.
Thus vanish sceptres, coronets, and balls,
And leave you in lone woods, or empty walls.
   So when your slave, at some dear, idle time,
(Not plagued with headaches, or the want of rhyme)
Stands in the streets, abstracted from the crew,
And while he seems to study, thinks of you:
Just when his fancy points your sprightly eyes,
Or sees the blush of soft Parthenia rise,
Gay pats my shoulder, and you vanish quite;
Streets, chairs, and coxcombs rush upon my sight;
Vexed to be still in town, I knit my brow,
Look sour, and hum a tune – as you may now.

Bohea one of the finest kinds of
   black tea
whisk whist

flirt a sudden movement of the
   fan
chairs sedan-chairs

Walter Savage Landor

WHAT NEWS

Here, ever since you went abroad,
   If there be change, no change I see,
I only walk our wonted road,
   The road is only walkt by me.

Yes; I forgot; a change there is;
    Was it of *that* you bade me tell?
I catch at times, at times I miss
    The sight, the tone, I know so well.

Only two months since you stood here!
    Two shortest months! then tell me why
Voices are harsher than they were,
    And tears are longer ere they dry.

Rihaku

THE RIVER-MERCHANT'S WIFE: A LETTER

While my hair was still cut straight across my forehead
I played about the front gate, pulling flowers.
You came by on bamboo stilts, playing horse,
You walked about my seat, playing with blue plums.
And we went on living in the village of Chokan:
Two small people, without dislike or suspicion.

At fourteen I married My Lord you.
I never laughed, being bashful.
Lowering my head, I looked at the wall.
Called to, a thousand times, I never looked back.

At fifteen I stopped scowling,
I desired my dust to be mingled with yours
For ever and for ever and for ever.
Why should I climb the look out?

At sixteen you departed,
You went into far Ku-to-yen, by the river of swirling
    eddies,
And you have been gone five months.
The monkeys make sorrowful noise overhead

You dragged your feet when you went out.
By the gate now, the moss is grown, the different mosses,
Too deep to clear them away!
The leaves fall early this autumn, in wind.
The paired butterflies are already yellow with August
Over the grass in the West garden;
They hurt me. I grow older.
If you are coming down through the narrows of the river
 Kiang,
Please let me know beforehand,
And I will come out to meet you
     As far as Cho-fu-Sa.

Translated from the Chinese by
Ezra Pound

Anon

TENTH CENTURY

THE WIFE'S COMPLAINT

I have wrought these words together out of a wryed
 existence,
the heart's tally, telling off
the griefs I have undergone from girlhood upwards,
old and new, and now more than ever;
for I have never not had some new sorrow,
some fresh affliction to fight against.

The first was my lord's leaving his people here:
crossed crests. To what country I knew not,
wondered where, awoke unhappy.
I left, fared any road, friendless, an outcast,
sought any service to staunch the lack of him.

257

Then his kinsmen ganged, began to think
thoughts they did not speak, of splitting the wedlock;
so — estranged, alienated — we lived each
alone, a long way apart; how I longed for him!

In his harshness he had me brought here;
and in these parts there were few friendly-minded,
worth trusting.
           Trouble in the heart now:
I saw the bitterness, the bound mind
of my matched man, mourning-browed,
mirk in his mood, murder in his thoughts.

Our lips had smiled to swear hourly
that nothing should split us — save dying —
nothing else. All that has changed:
it is now as if it never had been,
our friendship. I feel in the wind
that the man dearest to me detests me.
I was banished to this knoll knotted by woods
to live in a den dug beneath an oak.
Old is this earthen room; it eats at my heart.

I see the thorns thrive up there in thick coverts
on the banks that baulk these black hollows:
not a gay dwelling. Here the grief bred
by lordlack preys on me. Some lovers in this world
live dear to each other, lie warm together
at day's beginning; I go by myself
about these earth caves under the oak tree.
Here I must sit the summer day through,
here weep out the woes of exile,
the hardships heaped upon me. My heart shall never
suddenly sail into slack water,
all the longings of a lifetime answered.

May grief and bitterness blast the mind
of that young man! May his mind ache
behind his smiling face! May a flock of sorrows
choke his chest! He would change his tune
if he lived alone in a land of exile
far from his folk.

              Where my friend is stranded
frost crusts the cracked cliff-face
grey waves grind the shingle.
The mind cannot bear in such a bleak place
very much grief.

             He remembers too often
less grim surroundings. Sorrow follows
this too long wait for one who is estranged.

Translated from the Anglo-Saxon by
Michael Alexander

Ernest Dowson

EXILE

For CONAL HOLMES O'CONNELL O'RIORDAN

By the sad waters of separation
   Where we have wandered by divers ways,
I have but the shadow and imitation
   Of the old memorial days.

In music I have no consolation,
   No roses are pale enough for me;
The sound of the waters of separation
   Surpasseth roses and melody.

By the sad waters of separation
   Dimly I hear from an hidden place
The sigh of mine ancient adoration:
   Hardly can I remember your face.

If you be dead, no proclamation
   Sprang to me over the waste, gray sea:
Living, the waters of separation
   Sever for ever your soul from me.

No man knoweth our desolation;
   Memory pales of the old delight;
While the sad waters of separation
   Bear us on to the ultimate night.

Lady Heguri

A thousand years, you said,
as our hearts melted.
I look at the hand you held,
and the ache is hard to bear.

Translated from the Japanese by
Geoffrey Bownas and Anthony Thwaite

Christina Rossetti

REMEMBER

Remember me when I am gone away,
   Gone far away into the silent land;
   When you can no more hold me by the hand,
Nor I half turn to go, yet turning stay.
Remember me when no more day by day
   You tell me of our future that you planned:
   Only remember me; you understand
It will be late to counsel then or pray.

Yet if you should forget me for a while
   And afterwards remember, do not grieve:
   For if the darkness and corruption leave
   A vestige of the thoughts that once I had,
Better by far you should forget and smile
   Than that you should remember and be sad.

Christina Rossetti

SONG

When I am dead, my dearest,
   Sing no sad songs for me;
Plant thou no roses at my head,
   Nor shady cypress tree:
Be the green grass above me
   With showers and dewdrops wet;
And if thou wilt, remember,
   And if thou wilt, forget.

I shall not see the shadows,
   I shall not feel the rain;
I shall not hear the nightingale
   Sing on, as if in pain;
And dreaming through the twilight
   That doth not rise nor set,
Haply I may remember,
   And haply may forget.

Philip Bourke Marston

INSEPARABLE

When thou and I are dead, my dear,
   The earth above us lain;
When we no more in autumn hear
   The fall of leaves and rain,
Or round the snow-enshrouded year
   The midnight winds complain;

When we no more in green mid-spring,
   Its sights and sounds may mind, –
The warm wet leaves set quivering
   With touches of the wind,
The birds at morn, and birds that sing
   When day is left behind;

When, over all, the moonlight lies,
   Intensely bright and still;
When some meandering brooklet sighs
   At parting from its hill,
And scents from voiceless gardens rise,
   The peaceful air to fill;

When we no more through summer light
   The deep dim woods discern,
Nor hear the nightingales at night,
   In vehement singing, yearn
To stars and moon, that dumb and bright,
   In nightly vigil burn;

When smiles and hopes and joys and fears
   And words that lovers say,

And sighs of love, and passionate tears
    Are lost to us, for aye, –
What thing of all our love appears,
    In cold and coffined clay?

When all their kisses, sweet and close,
    Our lips shall quite forget;
When, where the day upon us rose,
    The day shall rise and set,
While we for love's sublime repose,
    Shall have not one regret, –

Oh, this true comfort is, I think,
    That, be death near or far,
When we have crossed the fatal brink,
    And found nor moon nor star,
We know not, when in death we sink,
    The lifeless things we are.

Yet one thought is, I deem, more kind,
    That when we sleep so well,
On memories that we leave behind
    When kindred souls shall dwell,
My name to thine in words they'll bind
    Of love inseparable.

E. E. Cummings

if i should sleep with a lady called death
get another man with firmer lips
to take your new mouth in his teeth
(hips pumping pleasure into hips).

263

Seeing how the limp huddling string
of your smile over his body squirms
kissingly, i will bring you every spring
handfuls of little normal worms.

Dress deftly your flesh in stupid stuffs,
phrase the immense weapon of your hair.
Understanding why his eye laughs,
i will bring you every year

something which is worth the whole,
an inch of nothing for your soul.

John Cornford

HUESCA

Heart of the heartless world,
Dear heart, the thought of you
Is the pain at my side,
The shadow that chills my view.

The wind rises in the evening,
Reminds that autumn is near.
I am afraid to lose you,
I am afraid of my fear.

On the last mile to Huesca,
The last fence for our pride,
Think so kindly, dear, that I
Sense you at my side.

And if bad luck should lay my strength
Into the shallow grave,
Remember all the good you can;
Don't forget my love.

Henry King

THE SURRENDER

My once dear love; hapless that I no more
Must call thee so: the rich affection's store
That fed our hopes, lies now exhaust and spent,
Like sums of treasure unto bankrupts lent.

We that did nothing study but the way
To love each other, with which thought the day
Rose with delight to us, and with them set,
Must learn the hateful art, how to forget.

We that did nothing wish that Heaven could give
Beyond ourselves, nor did desire to live
Beyond that wish, all these now cancel must,
As if not writ in faith, but words, and dust.

Yet witness those clear vows which lovers make!
Witness the chaste desires, that never brake
Into unruly heats; witness that breast
Which in thy bosom anchored his whole rest,
'Tis no default in us. I dare acquite
Thy maiden-faith, thy purpose fair and white
As thy pure self. Cross planets did envy
Us to each other, and Heaven did untie
Faster than vows could bind. O that the stars
When lovers meet, should stand opposed in wars!
Since then some higher destinies command
Let us not strive, nor labour to withstand
What is past help. The longest date of grief
Can never yield a hope of our relief.
And though we waste ourselves in moist laments,
Tears may drown us, but not our discontents.

Fold back our arms, take home our fruitless loves,
That must new fortunes try, like turtle doves

Dislodgèd from their haunts. We must in tears
Unwind a love knit up in many years.
In this last kiss I here surrender thee
Back to thyself. Lo thou again art free.
Thou in another, sad as that, resend
The truest heart that lover e'er did lend.
    Now turn from each. So fare our severed hearts
As the divorced soul from her body parts.

R. S. *Thomas*

MADRIGAL

Your love is dead, lady, your love is dead;
Dribbles no sound
From his stopped lips, though swift underground
Spurts his wild hair.

Your love is dead, lady, your love is dead;
Faithless he lies
Deaf to your call, though shades of his eyes
Break through and stare.

Luis de Camoëns

Dear gentle soul, who went so soon away
Departing from this life in discontent,
Repose in that far sky to which you went
While on this earth I linger in dismay.
In the ethereal seat where you must be,
If you consent to memories of our sphere,
Recall the love which, burning pure and clear,
So often in my eyes you used to see!

If then, in the incurable, long anguish
Of having lost you, as I pine and languish,
You see some merit – do this favour for me:
And to the God who cut your life short, pray
That he as early to your sight restore me
As from my own he swept you far away.

Translated from the Portuguese by
Roy Campbell

Lady Catherine Dyer

EPITAPH ON THE MONUMENT OF SIR WILLIAM DYER AT COLMWORTH, 1641

My dearest dust, could not thy hasty day
Afford thy drowsy patience leave to stay
One hour longer: so that we might either
Sit up, or gone to bed together?
But since thy finished labour hath possessed
Thy weary limbs with early rest,
Enjoy it sweetly: and thy widow bride
Shall soon repose her by thy slumbering side.
Whose business, now, is only to prepare
My nightly dress, and call to prayer:
Mine eyes wax heavy and the day grows cold.
Draw, draw the closèd curtains: and make room:
My dear, my dearest dust; I come, I come.

Henry King

EXEQUY ON HIS WIFE

Accept, thou shrine of my dead saint,
Instead of dirges this complaint;
And for sweet flowers to crown thy hearse,
Receive a strew of weeping verse
From thy grieved friend, whom thou mightst see
Quite melted into tears for thee.
   Dear loss! since thy untimely fate
My task hath been to meditate
On thee, on thee! Thou art the book,
The library, whereon I look
Though almost blind. For thee, loved clay,
I languish out, not live, the day,
Using no other exercise
But what I practise with mine eyes.
By which wet glasses I find out
How lazily time creeps about
To one that mourns. This, only this,
My exercise and business is:
So I compute the weary hours
With sighs dissolvèd into showers.
   Nor wonder if my time go thus
Backward and most preposterous:
Thou hast benighted me. Thy set
This eve of blackness did beget,
Who wast my day (though overcast
Before thou hadst thy noon-tide past)
And I remember must in tears
Thou scarce hadst seen so many years
As day tells hours. By thy clear sun
My love and fortune first did run;

But thou wilt never more appear
Folded within my hemisphere,
Since both thy light and motion,
Like a fled star, is fallen and gone,
And 'twixt me and my soul's dear wish
The earth now interposèd is,
Which such a strange eclipse doth make
As ne'er was read in almanac.

    I could allow thee for a time
To darken me and my sad clime;
Were it a month, a year, or ten,
I would thy exile live till then;
And all that space my mirth adjourn,
So thou wouldst promise to return
And, putting off thy ashy shroud,
At length disperse this sorrow's cloud.

    But woe is me! the longest date
Too narrow is to calculate
These empty hopes. Never shall I
Be so much blessed as to descry
A glimpse of thee, till that day come
Which shall the earth to cinders doom,
And a fierce fever must calcine
The body of this world, like thine,
My little world! That fit of fire
Once off, our bodies shall aspire
To our souls' bliss: then we shall rise,
And view ourselves with clearer eyes
In that calm region where no night
Can hide us from each other's sight.

    Meantime thou hast her, Earth: much good
May my harm do thee. Since it stood
With Heaven's will I might not call
Her longer mine, I give thee all

My short-lived right and interest
In her, whom living I loved best:
With a most free and bounteous grief,
I give thee what I could not keep.
Be kind to her, and prithee look
Thou write into thy Doomsday book
Each parcel of this rarity,
Which in thy casket shrined doth lie.
See that thou make thy reckoning straight,
And yield her back again by weight;
For thou must audit on thy trust
Each grain and atom of this dust,
As thou wilt answer him that lent,
Not gave thee, my dear monument.

So close the ground, and 'bout her shade
Black curtains draw: my bride is laid.

Sleep on, my Love, in thy cold bed
Never to be disquieted.
My last good night! Thou wilt not wake
Till I thy fate shall overtake:
Till age, or grief, or sickness must
Marry my body to that dust
It so much loves; and fill the room
My heart keeps empty in thy tomb.
Stay for me there: I will not fail
To meet thee in that hollow vale.
And think not much of my delay;
I am already on the way,
And follow thee with all the speed
Desire can make, or sorrows breed.
Each minute is a short degree
And every hour a step towards thee.
At night when I betake to rest,
Next morn I rise nearer my west

Of life, almost by eight hours sail
Than when sleep breathed his drowsy gale.
  Thus from the sun my bottom steers,
And my day's compass downward bears.
Nor labour I to stem the tide
Through which to thee I swiftly glide.
  'Tis true, with shame and grief I yield;
Thou, like the van, first took'st the field
And gotten hast the victory
In thus adventuring to die
Before me, whose more years might crave
A just precedence in the grave.
But hark! my pulse, like a soft drum,
Beats my approach, tells thee I come;
And slow howe'er my marches be
I shall at last sit down by thee.
  The thought of this bids me go on
And wait my dissolution
With hope and comfort. Dear, (forgive
The crime) I am content to live
Divided, with but half a heart,
Till we shall meet and never part.

John Milton

Methought I saw my late espousèd saint
  Brought to me like Alcestis from the grave,
  Whom Jove's great son to her glad husband gave,
  Rescued from death by force though pale and faint.
Mine as whom washed from spot of childbed taint,
  Purification in the old Law did save,
  And such, as yet once more I trust to have

Full sight of her in Heaven without restraint,
Came vested all in white, pure as her mind:
    Her face was veiled, yet to my fancied sight,
    Love, sweetness, goodness, in her person shined
So clear, as in no face with more delight.
    But O as to embrace me she inclined
    I waked, she fled, and day brought back my night.

Sir Henry Wotton

UPON THE DEATH OF
SIR ALBERT MORTON'S WIFE

He first deceased; she for a little tried
To live without him, liked it not, and died.

DESOLATIONS

Sappho

Mother, I cannot mind my wheel;
   My fingers ache, my lips are dry;
Oh! if you felt the pain I feel!
   But oh, who ever felt as I!

Translated from the Greek by
Walter Savage Landor

Sir Philip Sidney

With how sad steps, O moon, thou climb'st the skies!
How silently, and with how wan a face!
What! may it be that even in heavenly place
That busy archer his sharp arrows tries?
Sure, if that long-with-love-acquainted eyes
Can judge of love, thou feel'st a lover's case:
I read it in thy looks; thy languished grace
To me, that feel the like, thy state descries.
Then, even of fellowship, O Moon, tell me,
Is constant love deemed there but want of wit?
Are beauties there as proud as here they be?
Do they above love to be loved, and yet
   Those lovers scorn whom that love doth possess?
   Do they call 'virtue' there — ungratefulness?

Sir John Suckling

A DOUBT OF MARTYRDOM

O for some honest lover's ghost,
　　Some kind unbodied post
　　Sent from the shades below!
　　I strangely long to know
Whether the nobler chaplets wear
Those that their mistress' scorn did bear
　　Or those that were used kindly.

For whatso'er they tell us here
　　To make those sufferings dear,
　　'Twill there, I fear, be found
　　That to the being crowned
T' have loved alone will not suffice,
Unless we also have been wise
　　And have our loves enjoyed.

What posture can we think him in
　　That, here unloved, again
　　Departs, and's thither gone
　　Where each sits by his own?
Or how can that Elysium be
Where I my mistress still must see
　　Circled in other's arms?

For there the judges all are just,
　　And Sophonisba must
　　Be his whom she held dear,
　　Not his who loved her here.
The sweet Philoclea, since she died,
Lies by her Pirocles his side,
　　Not by Amphialus.

Some bays, perchance, or myrtle bough
　　For difference crowns the brow
　　Of those kind souls that were
　　The noble martyrs here;
And if that be the only odds
(As who can tell?), ye kinder gods,
　　Give me the woman here.

chaplets wreaths

Matthew Arnold

TO MARGUERITE – CONTINUED

Yes! in the sea of life enisled,
　With echoing straits between us thrown,
Dotting the shoreless watery wild,
　We mortal millions live *alone*.
The islands feel the enclasping flow,
And then their endless bounds they know.

But when the moon their hollows lights,
　And they are swept by balms of spring,
And in their glens, on starry nights,
　The nightingales divinely sing;
And lovely notes, from shore to shore,
Across the sounds and channels pour –

O! then a longing like despair
　Is to their farthest caverns sent;
For surely once, they feel, we were
　Parts of a single continent!
Now round us spreads the watery plain –
O might our marges meet again!

Who ordered that their longing's fire
　　Should be, as soon as kindled, cooled?
Who renders vain their deep desire? –
　　A God, a God their severance ruled!
And bade betwixt their shores to be
The unplumbed, salt, estranging sea.

Andrew Marvell

THE DEFINITION OF LOVE

My Love is of a birth as rare
As 'tis for object strange and high:
It was begotten by Despair
Upon Impossibility.

Magnanimous Despair alone
Could show me so divine a thing,
Where feeble Hope could ne'er have flown
But vainly flapped its tinsel wing.

And yet I quickly might arrive
Where my extended soul is fixed,
But Fate does iron wedges drive,
And always crowds itself betwixt.

For Fate with jealous eye does see
Two perfect Loves; nor lets them close:
Their union would her ruin be,
And her tyrannic power depose.

And therefore her decrees of steel
Us as the distant Poles have placed,
(Though Love's whole World on us doth wheel)
Not by themselves to be embraced.

Unless the giddy Heaven fall,
And Earth some new convulsion tear;
And, us to join, the World should all
Be cramped into a planisphere.

As lines so Love oblique may well
Themselves in every angle greet:
But ours so truly parallel,
Though infinite, can never meet.

Therefore the Love which us doth bind
But Fate so enviously debars,
Is the conjunction of the Mind,
And opposition of the Stars.

Petrarch

Whoso list to hunt, I know where is an hind,
  But as for me, alas, I may no more
  The vain travail hath wearied me so sore.
I am of them that farthest cometh behind;
Yet may I by no means my wearied mind
  Draw from the Deer: but as she fleeth afore,
  Fainting I follow. I leave off therefore,
Since in a net I seek to hold the wind.
Who list her hunt, I put him out of doubt,
  As well as I may spend his time in vain:
  And, graven with diamonds, in letters plain
There is written her fair neck round about:
  Noli me tangere, for Caesar's I am;
  And wild for to hold, though I seem tame.

Translated from the Italian by
Sir Thomas Wyatt

Sir Thomas Wyatt

I abide and abide and better abide
(And after the old proverb) the happy day;
And ever my lady to me doth say
'Let me alone and I will provide'.
I abide and abide and tarry the tide,
And with abiding speed well ye may!
Thus do I abide I wot alway
Not her obtaining nor yet denied.
Aye me! this long abiding
Seemeth to me as who sayeth
A prolonging of a dying death
Or a refusing of a desired thing.
Much were it better for to be plain
Than to say 'abide' and yet not obtain.

Thomas Campion

Kind are her answers,
But her performance keeps no day;
Breaks time, as dancers
From their own music when they stray:
All her free favours
And smooth words wing my hopes in vain.
O did ever voice so sweet but only feign?
Can true love yield such delay,
Converting joy to pain?

Lost is our freedom,
When we submit to women so:
Why do we need 'em,
When in their best they work our woe?

There is no wisdom
Can alter ends, by Fate prefixed.
O why is the good of man with evil mixed?
    Never were days yet called two,
    But one night went betwixt.

Catullus

Lesbia loads me night & day with her curses,
'Catullus' always on her lips,
        yet I know that she loves me.
How? I equally spend myself day & night
in assiduous execration
        – knowing too well my hopeless love.

Translated from the Latin by
Peter Whigham

Meleager

Busy with love, the bumble bee
philanders through the petalled spring
& lights on Heliodora's skin.

And have you left the stamen-cup
to tell me Cupid's arrow stings?
till rueful Heart heaves up:

                'Enough'?
Thou loved of lovers, Bee, buzz off –
what zestful petals wait your tupping!
Such news to me was never new
whose honey's long been mixed with rue.

Translated from the Greek by
Peter Whigham

William Blake

MY PRETTY ROSE TREE

A flower was offered to me,
Such a flower as May never bore;
But I said 'I've a Pretty Rose-tree,'
And I passed the sweet flower o'er.

Then I went to my Pretty Rose-tree,
To tend her by day and by night;
But my Rose turned away with jealousy,
And her thorns were my only delight.

William Walsh

LOVE AND JEALOUSY

How much are they deceived who vainly strive,
By jealous fears, to keep our flames alive?
Love's like a torch, which if secured from blasts,
Will faintlier burn; but then it longer lasts.
Exposed to storms of jealousy and doubt,
The blaze grows greater, but 'tis sooner out.

Sir John Suckling

SONG

Why so pale and wan, fond lover?
    Prithee, why so pale?
Will, when looking well can't move her,
    Looking ill prevail?
    Prithee, why so pale?

Why so dull and mute, young sinner?
    Prithee, why so mute?
Will, when speaking well can't win her,
    Saying nothing do 't?
    Prithee, why so mute?

Quit, quit for shame! This will not move;
    This cannot take her.
If of herself she will not love,
    Nothing can make her:
    The devil take her.

Tony Connor

APOLOGUE

Having a fine new suit,
and no invitations,
I slept in my new suit
hoping to induce
a dream of fair women.

And did indeed: the whole night long,
implored by naked
beauty – pink on white linen –
I struggled to remove
my fine new suit.

At dawn I awoke, blear-eyed;
sweating beneath encumbering rags.

283

Donald Justice

IN BERTRAM'S GARDEN

Jane looks down at her organdy skirt
As if *it* somehow were the thing disgraced,
For being there, on the floor, in the dirt,
And she catches it up about her waist,
Smooths it out along one hip,
And pulls it over the crumpled slip.

On the porch, green-shuttered, cool,
Asleep is Bertram, that bronze boy,
Who, having wound her around a spool,
Sends her spinning like a toy
Out to the garden, all alone,
To sit and weep on a bench of stone.

Soon the purple dark must bruise
Lily and bleeding-heart and rose,
And the little Cupid lose
Eyes and ears and chin and nose,
And Jane lie down with others soon,
Naked to the naked moon.

Louis MacNeice

CHRISTINA

It all began so easy
With bricks upon the floor
Building motley houses
And knocking down your houses
And always building more.

The doll was called Christina,
Her under-wear was lace,
She smiled while you dressed her
And when you then undressed her
She kept a smiling face.

Until the day she tumbled
And broke herself in two
And her legs and arms were hollow
And her yellow head was hollow
Behind her eyes of blue.

.   .   .   .   .

He went to bed with a lady
Somewhere seen before,
He heard the name Christina
And suddenly saw Christina
Dead on the nursery floor.

Oliver Goldsmith

SONG

When lovely woman stoops to folly,
    And finds too late that men betray,
What charm can soothe her melancholy;
    What art can wash her guilt away?

The only art her guilt to cover,
    To hide her shame from every eye,
To give repentance to her lover,
    And wring his bosom – is to die.

John Dryden

Farewell ungrateful traitor,
    Farewell my perjured swain,
Let never injured creature
    Believe a man again.
The pleasure of possessing
Surpasses all expressing,
But 'tis too short a blessing,
    And love too long a pain.

'Tis easy to deceive us
    In pity of your pain,
But when we love you leave us
    To rail at you in vain.
Before we have descried it,
There is no bliss beside it,
But she that once has tried it
    Will never love again.

The passion you pretended
    Was only to obtain,
But when the charm is ended
    The charmer you disdain.
Your love by ours we measure
Till we have lost our treasure,
But dying is a pleasure,
    When living is a pain.

Anon

SEVENTEENTH CENTURY

Oh! the time that is past,
    When she held me so fast,
And declared that her honour no longer could last:
No light but her languishing eyes did appear,
To prevent all excuses of blushing and fear.

When she sighed and unlaced
    With such trembling and haste,
As if she had longed to be closer embraced!
My lips the sweet pleasure of kisses enjoyed,
While my hands were in search of hid treasure employed.

With my heart all on fire
    In the flames of desire,
I boldly pursued what she seemed to require:
She cried: *Oh, for pity's sake! change your ill mind:*
Pray, Amyntas, be civil, or I'll be unkind.

All your bliss you destroy,
    Like a naked young boy,
Who fears the kind river he came to enjoy . . .
Let's in, my dear Cloris! I'll save thee from harm,
And make the cold element pleasant and warm.

Dear Amyntas! she cries;
    Then she casts down her eyes,
And with kisses consents what she faintly denies:
Too sure of my conquest, I purpose to stay
Till her freer consent did more sweeten the prey.

But too late I begun;
   For her passion was done:
Now, Amyntas, she cries, I will never be won:
Thy tears and thy courtship no pity can move;
Thou hast slighted the critical minute of love.

Charles Baudelaire

DAMNED WOMEN

DELPHINE AND HIPPOLYTA

Over deep cushions, drenched with drowsy scents
Where fading lamplight shed its dying glow,
Hippolyta recalls and half-repents
The kisses that first thawed her youthful snow.

She sought, with tempest-troubled gaze, the skies
Of her first innocence, now far away,
As travellers who backward turn their eyes
To blue horizons passed at break of day.

Within her haggard eyes the tears were bright.
Her broken look, her dazed, voluptuous air,
Her vanquished arms like weapons shed in flight,
Enhanced her fragile beauty with despair.

Stretched at her feet Delphine contented lay
And watched with burning eyeballs from beneath
Like a fierce tigress who, to guard her prey,
Has set a mark upon it with her teeth.

Strong beauty there to fragile beauty kneeling,
Superb, she seemed to sniff the heady wine
Of triumph: and stretched out to her, appealing
For the reward of raptures half-divine.

She sought within her victim's pallid eye
Dumb hymns that pleasure sings without a choir,
And gratitude that, like a long-drawn sigh,
Swells from the eyelid, swooning with fire.

'Hippolyta, dear heart, have you no trust?
Do you not know the folly that exposes
To the fierce pillage of the brawling gust
The sacred holocaust of early roses?

My kisses are as light as fairy midges
That on calm evenings skim the crystal lake.
Those of your man would plough such ruts and ridges
As lumbering carts or tearing coulters make.

They'll tramp across you, like a ruthless team
Of buffaloes or horses, yoked in lust.
Dear sister, turn your face to me, my dream,
My soul, my all, my twin, to whom I trust!

Turn me your eyes of deepest, starry blue.
For one of those deep glances that you send,
I'd lift the veil of darkest joys for you
And rock you in a dream that has no end.'

But then Hippolyta raised up her head,
'No blame nor base ingratitude I feel,
But, as it were, a kind of nauseous dread
After some terrible, nocturnal meal.

I feel a swooping terror that explodes
In legions of black ghosts towards me speeding
Who crowd me on to swiftly moving roads,
That, sliced by sheer horizons, end up bleeding.

Have we done something monstrous that I tremble?
Explain, then, if you can; for when you say,
'Angel', I cower. Yet I cannot dissemble
That, when you speak, my lips are drawn your way.

Oh, do not fix me with a stare so steady
You whom I love till death in still submission,
Yes, even though you, like an ambush ready,
Are the beginning of my own perdition.'

Then Delphine stamped and shook her tragic mane,
And, like a priestess, foaming and fierce, and fell,
Spoke in a lordly and prophetic strain
— 'Who dares, in front of Love, to mention Hell?

Curbed forever be that useless dreamer
Who first imagined, in his brutish mind,
Of sheer futility the fatuous schemer,
Honour with Love could ever be combined.

He who in mystic union would enmesh
Shadow with warmth, and daytime with the night,
Will never warm his paralytic flesh
At the red sun of amorous delight.

Go, if you wish, and seek some boorish lover:
Offer your virgin heart to his crude hold,
Full of remorse and horror you'll recover,
And bring me your scarred breast to be consoled . . .

Down here, a soul can only serve one master.'
But the girl, venting her tremendous woe,
Cried out 'I feel a huge pit of disaster
Yawning within: it is my heart, I know!

Like a volcano burning, deep as death,
There's naught that groaning monster can assuage
Nor quench of thirst the Fury's burning breath
Who brands it with a torch to make it rage.

Let our closed curtains isolate the rest,
Until exhaustion bring us sleep, while I
Annihilate myself upon your breast
And find in you a tomb on which to die.'

Go down, go down, poor victims, it is time;
The road to endless hell awaits your lusts.
Plunge to the bottom of the gulf, where crime
Is flagellated by infernal gusts.

Swirling pell-mell, and with a tempest's roar,
Mad shades, pursue your craving without measure:
Your rages will be sated nevermore,
Your torture is begotten of your pleasure.

No sunbeam through your dungeon will come leaking:
Only miasmic fevers, through each chink,
Will filter, like sick lanterns, redly streaking,
And penetrate your bodies with their stink.

The harsh sterility of all you relish
Will swell your thirst, and turn you both to hags.
The wind of your desire, with fury hellish
Will flog your flapping carrion like wet flags.

Far from live folk, like werewolves howling high,
Gallop the boundless deserts you unroll.
Fulfil your doom, disordered minds, and fly
The infinite you carry in your soul.

Translated from the French by
Roy Campbell

A. E. Housman

When I was one-and-twenty
  I heard a wise man say,
'Give crowns and pounds and guineas
  But not your heart away;
Give pearls away and rubies
  But keep your fancy free.'
But I was one-and-twenty,
  No use to talk to me.

When I was one-and-twenty
  I heard him say again,
'The heart out of the bosom
  Was never given in vain;
'Tis paid with sighs a plenty
  And sold for endless rue.'
And I am two-and-twenty,
  And oh, 'tis true, 'tis true.

W. B. Yeats

NEVER GIVE ALL THE HEART

Never give all the heart, for love
Will hardly seem worth thinking of
To passionate women if it seem
Certain, and they never dream
That it fades out from kiss to kiss;
For everything that's lovely is
But a brief, dreamy, kind delight.
O never give the heart outright,

For they, for all smooth lips can say,
Have given their hearts up to the play.
And who could play it well enough
If deaf and dumb and blind with love?
He that made this knows all the cost,
For he gave all his heart and lost.

Christina Rossetti

MIRAGE

The hope I dreamed of was a dream,
　　Was but a dream; and now I wake,
Exceeding comfortless, and worn, and old,
　　For a dream's sake.

I hang my harp upon a tree,
　　A weeping willow in a lake;
I hang my silenced harp there, wrung and snapt
　　For a dream's sake.

Lie still, lie still, my breaking heart;
　　My silent heart, lie still and break:
Life, and the world, and mine own self, are changed
　　For a dream's sake.

Robert Burns

THE BANKS O' DOON

Ye flowery banks o' bonie Doon,
　　How can ye blume sae fair;
How can ye chant, ye little birds,
　　And I sae fu' o' care!

Thou'll break my heart, thou bonie bird
    That sings upon the bough;
Thou minds me o' the happy days
    When my fause luve was true.

Thou'll break my heart, thou bonie bird
    That sings beside thy mate;
For sae I sat, and sae I sang,
    And wist na o' my fate.

Aft hae I rov'd by bonie Doon,
    To see the wood-bine twine,
And ilka bird sang o' its love,
    And sae did I o' mine.

Wi' lightsome heart I pu'd a rose
    Frae aff its thorny tree,
And my fause luver staw the rose,
    But left the thorn wi' me.

Wi' lightsome heart I pu'd a rose,
    Upon a morn in June:
And sae I flourish'd on the morn,
    And sae was pu'd or noon!

William Blake

THE SICK ROSE

O Rose, thou art sick!
The invisible worm
That flies in the night,
In the howling storm,

Has found out thy bed
Of crimson joy:
And his dark secret love
Does thy life destroy.

Sir Walter Ralegh

A FAREWELL TO FALSE LOVE

Farewell false love, the oracle of lies,
A mortal foe and enemy to rest:
An envious boy, from whom all cares arise,
A bastard vile, a beast with rage possessed:
A way of error, a temple full of treason,
In all effects, contrary unto reason.

A poisoned serpent covered all with flowers,
Mother of sighs, and murderer of repose,
A sea of sorrows from whence are drawn such showers
As moisture lend to every grief that grows,
A school of guile, a net of deep deceit,
A gilded hook, that holds a poisoned bait.

A fortress foiled, which reason did defend,
A Siren song, a fever of the mind,
A maze wherein affection finds no end,
A ranging cloud that runs before the wind,
A substance like the shadow of the sun,
A goal of grief for which the wisest run.

A quenchless fire, a nurse of trembling fear,
A path that leads to peril and mishap,
A true retreat of sorrow and despair,
An idle boy that sleeps in pleasure's lap,
A deep mistrust of that which certain seems,
A hope of that which reason doubtful deems.

Sith then thy trains my younger years betrayed
And for my faith ingratitude I find.
And sith repentance hath my wrongs bewrayed
Whose course was ever contrary to kind.
False Love; Desire; and Beauty frail adieu
Dead is the root whence all these fancies grew.

Yehuda Amichai

QUICK AND BITTER

The end was quick and bitter.
Slow and sweet was the time between us,
Slow and sweet were the nights
When my hands did not touch one another in despair
But with the love of your body
Which came between them.

And when I entered into you
It seemed then that great happiness
Could be measured with the precision
Of sharp pain. Quick and bitter.

Slow and sweet were the nights.
Now is as bitter and grinding as sand –
'We shall be sensible' and similar curses.

And as we stray further from love
We multiply the words,
Words and sentences long and orderly.
Had we remained together
We could have become a silence.

Translated from the Hebrew by
Assia Gutmann

Dante Gabriel Rossetti

from THE HOUSE OF LIFE

SEVERED SELVES

Two separate divided silences,
   Which, brought together, would find loving voice;
   Two glances which together would rejoice
In love, now lost like stars beyond dark trees;
Two hands apart whose touch alone gives ease;
   Two bosoms which, heart-shrined with mutual flame,
   Would, meeting in one clasp, be made the same;
Two souls, the shores wave mocked of sundering seas: –

Such are we now. Ah! may our hope forecast
   Indeed one hour again, when on this stream
   Of darkened love once more the light shall gleam? –
An hour how slow to come, how quickly past, –
Which blooms and fades, and only leaves at last,
   Faint as shed flowers, the attenuated dream.

W. D. Snodgrass

NO USE

No doubt this way is best.
No doubt in time I'd learn
To hate you like the rest
I once loved. Like an old
Shirt we unstitch and turn
Until it's all used out,
This too would turn cold.
     No doubt . . . no doubt . . .

And yet who'd dare think so
And yet dare think? We've been
Through all this; we should know
That man the gods have curst
Can ask and always win
Love, as castaways get
Whole seas to cure their thirst.
      And yet . . . and yet . . .

No use telling us love's
No use. Parched, cracked, the heart
Drains that love it loves
And still thirsts. We still care;
We're spared *that*. We're apart.
Tell me there's no excuse,
No sense to this despair. . . .
      No use . . . No use . . .

Hugh MacDiarmid

O WHA'S THE BRIDE?

O wha's the bride that cairries the bunch
O' thistles blinterin' white?
Her cuckold bridegroom little dreids
What he sall ken this nicht.

For closer than gudeman can come
And closer to'r than hersel',
Wha didna need her maidenheid
Has wrocht his purpose fell.

O wha's been here afore me, lass,
And hoo did he get in?
— *A man that deed or was I born*
This evil thing has din.

298

And left, as it were on a corpse,
Your maidenheid to me?
— *Nae lass, gudeman, sin' Time began*
'S hed ony mair to gi'e.

But I can gi'e ye kindness, lad,
And a pair o' willin' hands,
And you shall he'e my breists like stars,
My limbs like willow wands.

And on my lips ye'll heed nae mair,
And in my hair forget,
The seed o' a' the men that in
My virgin womb ha'e met. . . . .

blintering glimmering
dreids foresees
wrocht wraught, worked
deed died

or before
'S *hed ony mair to gi'e* has
had any more to give

Charlotte Mew

THE FARMER'S BRIDE

Three summers since I chose a maid,
Too young maybe — but more's to do
At harvest-time than bide and woo.
 When us was wed she turned afraid
Of love and me and all things human;
Like the shut of a winter's day
Her smile went out, and 'twadn't a woman —
 More like a little frightened fay.
 One night, in the Fall, she runned away.

'Out 'mong the sheep, her be,' they said,
'Should properly have been abed;
But sure enough she wadn't there
Lying awake with her wide brown stare.
Over seven-acre field and up-along across the down
We chased her, flying like a hare
Before our lanterns. To Church-Town
 All in a shiver and a scare
We caught her, fetched her home at last
 And turned the key upon her, fast.

She does the work about the house
As well as most, but like a mouse:
 Happy enough to chat and play
 With birds and rabbits and such as they,
 So long as men-folk keep away.

'Not near, not near!' her eyes beseech
When one of us comes within reach.
 The women say that beasts in stall
 Look round like children at her call.
 I've hardly heard her speak at all.

Shy as a leveret, swift as he,
Straight and slight as a young larch tree,
Sweet as the first wild violets, she,
To her wild self. But what to me?

The short days shorten and the oaks are brown,
 The blue smoke rises to the low grey sky,
One leaf in the still air falls slowly down,
 A magpie's spotted feathers lie
On the black earth spread white with rime,
The berries redden up to Christmas-time.
 What's Christmas-time without there be
 Some other in the house than we!

She sleeps up in the attic there
　　Alone, poor maid. 'Tis but a stair
Betwixt us. Oh! my God! the down,
　The soft young down of her, the brown,
The brown of her – her eyes, her hair, her hair!

Louis MacNeice

LES SYLPHIDES

Life in a day: he took his girl to the ballet;
Being shortsighted himself could hardly see it –
　　The white skirts in the grey
　　Glade and the swell of the music
　　Lifting the white sails.

Calyx upon calyx, canterbury bells in the breeze
The flowers on the left mirror to the flowers on the right
　　And the naked arms above
　　The powdered faces moving
　　Like seaweed in a pool.

Now, he thought, we are floating – ageless, oarless –
Now there is no separation, from now on
　　You will be wearing white
　　Satin and a red sash
　　Under the waltzing trees.

But the music stopped, the dancers took their curtain,
The river had come to a lock – a shuffle of programmes –
　　And we cannot continue down
　　Stream unless we are ready
　　To enter the lock and drop.

So they were married – to be the more together –
And found they were never again so much together,
    Divided by the morning tea,
    By the evening paper,
    By children and tradesmen's bills.

Waking at times in the night she found assurance
In his regular breathing but wondered whether
    It was really worth it and where
    The river had flowed away
    And where were the white flowers.

Jonathan Price

A CONSIDERED REPLY TO A CHILD

'I love you,' you said between two mouthfuls of pudding.
But not funny; I didn't want to laugh at all.
Rolling three years' experience in a ball,
You nudged it friendlily across the table.

A stranger, almost, I was flattered – no kidding.
It's not every day I hear a thing like that;
And when I do my answer's never pat.
I'm about nine times your age, ten times less able

To say – what you said; incapable of unloading
Plonk at someone's feet, like a box of bricks,
A declaration. When I try, it sticks
Like fish-bones in my throat; my eyes tingle.

What's called 'passion', you'll learn, may become
    'overriding'.
But not in me it doesn't: I'm that smart,
I can give everything and keep my heart.
Kisses are kisses. No need for souls to mingle.

Bed's bed, what's more, and you'd say it's meant for
    sleeping;
And, believe me, you'd be absolutely right.
With luck you'll never lie awake all night,
Someone beside you (rather like 'crying') weeping.

Philip Larkin

TALKING IN BED

Talking in bed ought to be easiest,
Lying together there goes back so far,
An emblem of two people being honest.

Yet more and more time passes silently.
Outside, the wind's incomplete unrest
Builds and disperses clouds about the sky,

And dark towns heap up on the horizon.
None of this cares for us. Nothing shows why
At this unique distance from isolation

It becomes still more difficult to find
Words at once true and kind,
Or not untrue and not unkind.

Edward Thomas

AND YOU, HELEN

And you, Helen, what should I give you?
So many things I would give you
Had I an infinite great store
Offered me and I stood before
To choose. I would give you youth,
All kinds of loveliness and truth.

A clear eye as good as mine,
Lands, waters, flowers, wine,
As many children as your heart
Might wish for, a far better art
Than mine can be, all you have lost
Upon the travelling waters tossed,
Or given to me. If I could choose
Freely in that great treasure-house
Anything from any shelf,
I would give you back yourself,
And power to discriminate
What you want and want it not too late,
Many fair days free from care
And heart to enjoy both foul and fair,
And myself, too, if I could find
Where it lay hidden and it proved kind.

George Meredith

from MODERN LOVE

In our old shipwrecked days there was an hour,
When in the firelight steadily aglow,
Joined slackly, we beheld the red chasm grow
Among the clicking coals. Our library-bower
That eve was left to us: and hushed we sat
As lovers to whom Time is whispering.
From sudden-opened doors we heard them sing:
The nodding elders mixed good wine with chat.
Well knew we that Life's greatest treasure lay
With us, and of it was our talk. 'Ah, yes!
Love dies!' I said: I never thought it less.
She yearned to me that sentence to unsay.

Then when the fire domed blackening, I found
Her cheek was salt against my kiss, and swift
Up the sharp scale of sobs her breast did lift: —
Now am I haunted by that taste! that sound!

At dinner, she is hostess, I am host.
Went the feast ever cheerfuller? She keeps
The Topic over intellectual deeps
In buoyancy afloat. They see no ghost.
With sparkling surface-eyes we ply the ball:
It is in truth a most contagious game:
HIDING THE SKELETON, shall be its name.
Such play as this the devils might appal!
But here's the greater wonder: in that we,
Enamoured of an acting nought can tire,
Each other, like true hypocrites, admire;
Warm-lighted looks, Love's ephemerioe,
Shoot gaily o'er the dishes and the wine.
We waken envy of our happy lot.
Fast, sweet, and golden, shows the marriage-knot.
Dear guests, you now have seen Love's corpse-light shine.

George Macdonald

A MAMMON-MARRIAGE

The croak of a raven hoar!
    A dog's howl, kennel-tied!
Loud shuts the carriage-door:
    The two are away on their ghastly ride
To Death's salt shore!

Where are the love and the grace?
    The bridegroom is thirsty and cold!

The bride's skull sharpens her face!
　　But the coachman is driving, jubilant, bold,
The devil's pace.

The horses shivered and shook
　　Waiting gaunt and haggard
With sorry and evil look
　　But swift as a drunken wind they staggered
'Longst Lethe brook.

Long since, they ran no more;
　　Heavily pulling they died
On the sand of the hopeless shore
　　Where never swelled or sank a tide,
And the salt burns sore.

Flat their skeletons lie,
　　White shadows on shining sand;
The crusted reins go high
　　To the crumbling coachman's bony hand
On his knees awry.

Side by side, jarring no more,
　　Day and night side by side,
Each by a doorless door,
　　Motionless sit the bridegroom and bride
On the Dead-Sea-shore.

Robert Graves

CALL IT A GOOD MARRIAGE

Call it a good marriage –
For no one ever questioned
Her warmth, his masculinity,
Their interlocking views;
Except one stray graphologist
Who frowned in speculation
At her h's and her s's,
His p's and w's.

Though few would still subscribe
To the monogamic axiom
That strife below the hip-bones
Need not estrange the heart,
Call it a good marriage:
More drew those two together,
Despite a lack of children,
Than pulled them apart.

Call it a good marriage:
They never fought in public,
They acted circumspectly
And faced the world with pride;
Thus the hazards of their love-bed
Were none of our damned business –
Till as jurymen we sat on
Two deaths by suicide.

Thomas Hardy

THE NEWCOMER'S WIFE

He paused on the sill of a door ajar
That screened a lively liquor-bar,
For the name had reached him through the door
Of her he had married the week before.

'We called her the Hack of the Parade;
But she was discreet in the games she played;
If slightly worn, she's pretty yet,
And gossips, after all, forget:

'And he knows nothing of her past;
I am glad the girl's in luck at last;
Such ones, though stale to native eyes,
Newcomers snatch at as a prize.'

'Yes, being a stranger he sees her blent
Of all that's fresh and innocent,
Nor dreams how many a love-campaign
She had enjoyed before his reign!'

That night there was the splash of a fall
Over the slimy harbour-wall:
They searched, and at the deepest place
Found him with crabs upon his face.

Anon

BONNY BARBARA ALLAN

It was in and about the Martinmas time,
　When the green leaves were a-falling,
That Sir John Graeme in the west country
　Fell in love with Barbara Allan.

He sent his man down through the town,
　To the place where she was dwelling,
O haste, and come to my master dear,
　Gin ye be Barbara Allan.

O hooly, hooly rose she up,
　To the place where he was lying,
And when she drew the curtain by,
　Young man, I think you're dying.

O it's I'm sick, and very very sick,
　And 'tis a' for Barbara Allan.
O the better for me ye's never be,
　Tho' your heart's blood were a-spilling.

O dinna ye mind, young man, said she,
　When ye was in the tavern a-drinking,
That ye made the healths gae round and round,
　And slighted Barbara Allan?

He turn'd his face unto the wall,
　And death was with him dealing;
Adieu, adieu, my dear friends all,
　And be kind to Barbara Allan.

And slowly, slowly raise she up,
   And slowly, slowly left him;
And sighing, said, she cou'd not stay,
   Since death of life had reft him.

She had not gane a mile but twa,
   When she heard the dead-bell ringing,
And every jow that the dead-bell gied,
   It cry'd, Wo to Barbara Allan.

O mother, mother, make my bed,
   O make it saft and narrow,
Since my love dy'd for me today,
   I'll die for him to-morrow.

hooly gently, softly   *dinna ye mind* don't you
jow toll   remember
gied gave

Mary Coleridge

'MY TRUE LOVE HATH MY HEART AND I HAVE HIS'

None ever was in love with me but grief.
   She wooed me from the day that I was born;
She stole my playthings first, the jealous thief,
   And left me there forlorn.

The birds that in my garden would have sung,
   She scared away with her unending moan;
She slew my lovers too when I was young,
   And left me there alone.

Grief, I have cursed thee often – now at last
　To hate thy name I am no longer free;
Caught in thy bony arms and prisoned fast,
　I love no love but thee.

Thomas Hardy

BEREFT

In the black winter morning
No light will be struck near my eyes
While the clock in the stairway is warning
For five, when he used to rise.
　　　Leave the door unbarred,
　　　The clock unwound.
　　　Make my lone bed hard –
　　　Would 'twere underground!

When the summer dawns clearly,
And the appletree-tops seem alight,
Who will undraw the curtain and cheerly
Call out that the morning is bright?

When I tarry at market
No form will cross Durnover Lea
In the gathering darkness, to hark at
Grey's Bridge for the pit-pat o' me.

When the supper crock's steaming,
And the time is the time of his tread,
I shall sit by the fire and wait dreaming
In a silence as of the dead.
　　　Leave the door unbarred,
　　　The clock unwound,
　　　Make my lone bed hard –
　　　Would 'twere underground!

Francis William Bourdillon

The night has a thousand eyes,
   And the day but one;
Yet the light of the bright world dies
   With the dying sun.

The mind has a thousand eyes,
   And the heart but one;
Yet the light of a whole life dies
   When love is done.

REVERBERATIONS

W. B. Yeats

WHEN YOU ARE OLD

When you are old and grey and full of sleep,
And nodding by the fire, take down this book,
And slowly read, and dream of the soft look
Your eyes had once, and of their shadows deep;

How many loved your moments of glad grace,
And loved your beauty with love false or true,
But one man loved the pilgrim soul in you,
And loved the sorrows of your changing face;

And bending down beside the glowing bars,
Murmur, a little sadly, how Love fled
And paced upon the mountains overhead
And hid his face amid a crowd of stars.

Robert Burns

SONG

It was upon a Lammas night,
    When corn rigs are bonie,
Beneath the moon's unclouded light,
    I held awa to Annie:
The time flew by, wi' tentless heed,
    Till 'tween the late and early;
Wi' sma' persuasion she agreed,
    To see me thro' the barley.

The sky was blue, the wind was still,
　The moon was shining clearly;
I set her down, wi' right good will,
　Amang the rigs o' barley:
I ken't her heart was a' my ain;
　I lov'd her most sincerely;
I kiss'd her owre and owre again,
　Amang the rigs o' barley.

I lock'd her in my fond embrace;
　Her heart was beating rarely:
My blessings on that happy place,
　Amang the rigs o' barley!
But by the moon and stars so bright,
　That shone that hour so clearly!
She ay shall bless that happy night,
　Amang the rigs o' barley.

I hae been blythe wi' Comrades dear;
　I hae been merry drinking;
I hae been joyfu' gath'rin gear;
　I hae been happy thinking:
But a' the pleasures e'er I saw,
　Tho' three times doubl'd fairly,
That happy night was worth them a',
　Amang the rigs o' barley.

CHORUS

Corn rigs, an' barley rigs,
　An' corn rigs are bonie:
I'll ne'er forget that happy night,
　Amang the rigs wi' Annie.

Paul Éluard

CURFEW

What else could we do, for the doors were guarded,
What else could we do, for they had imprisoned us,
What else could we do, for the streets were forbidden us,
What else could we do, for the town was asleep?
What else could we do, for she hungered and thirsted,
What else could we do, for we were defenceless,
What else could we do, for night had descended,
What else could we do, for we were in love?

*Translated from the French by
Quentin Stevenson*

W. B. Yeats

WHENCE HAD THEY COME?

Eternity is passion, girl or boy
Cry at the onset of their sexual joy
'For ever and for ever'; then awake
Ignorant what Dramatis Personae spake;
A passion-driven exultant man sings out
Sentences that he has never thought;
The Flagellant lashes those submissive loins
Ignorant what that dramatist enjoins,
What master made the lash. Whence had they come,
The hand and lash that beat down frigid Rome?
What sacred drama through her body heaved
When world-transforming Charlemagne was conceived?

Robert Graves

NEVER SUCH LOVE

Twined together and, as is customary,
For words of rapture groping, they
'Never such love,' swore, 'ever before was!'
Contrast with all loves that had failed or staled
Registered their own as love indeed.

And was this not to blab idly
The heart's fated inconstancy?
Better in love to seal the love-sure lips,
For truly love was before words were,
And no word given, no word broken.

When the name 'love' is uttered
(Love, the near-honourable malady
With which in greed and haste they
Each other do infect and curse)
Or, worse, is written down. . .

Wise after the event, by love withered,
A 'never more!' most frantically
Sorrow and shame would proclaim
Such as, they'd swear, never before were:
True lovers even in this.

Meleager

Love's night & a lamp
judged our vows:
that she would love me ever
& I should never leave her.
Love's night & you, lamp,
witnessed the pact.

Today the vow runs:
'Oaths such as these, water-words'.
Tonight, lamp,
witness her lying
         – in other arms.

Translated from the Greek by
Peter Whigham

Hedylos

SEDUCED GIRL

With wine and words of love and every vow
   He lulled me into bed and closed my eyes,
A sleepy, stupid innocent . . . So now
   I dedicate the spoils of my surprise:
The silk that bound my breasts, my virgin zone,
   The cherished purity I could not keep.
Goddess, remember we were all alone,
   And he was strong – and I was half asleep.

Translated from the Greek by
Louis Untermeyer

Maturai Eṛuttāḷaṉ Cēntampūtaṉ

WHAT SHE SAID

Before I laughed with him
    nightly,

      the slow waves beating
      on his wide shores
      and the palmyra
      bringing forth heron-like flowers
      near the waters,

my eyes were like the lotus
my arms had the grace of the bamboo
my forehead was mistaken for the moon.

      But now

*Translated from the Tamil b[
A. K. Ramanujan*

Alexander Scott

A RONDEL OF LOVE

Lo, quhat it is to love,
Learn ye that list to prove,
By me, I say, that no ways may
The grund of grief remove,
Bot still decay, both nicht and day;
Lo, quhat it is to love!

320

Love is ane fervent fire
Kindled without desire:
Short pleasure, lang displeasure,
Repentance is the hire;
Ane pure treasure without measure;
Love is ane fervent fire.

To love and to be wise,
To rage with gud adwyiss,
Now thus, now than, so goes the game,
Incertain is the dice:
There is no man, I say, that can
Both love and to be wise.

Flee always from the snare,
Learn at me to be ware;
It is ane pain, and double train
Of endless woe and care;
For to refrain that danger plain,
Flee always from the snare.

without measure of no account   *adwyiss* deliberation
train snare

George Granville, Baron Lansdowne

LOVE

Love is begot by fancy, bred
By ignorance, by expectation fed,
Destroyed by knowledge, and, at best,
Lost in the moment 'tis possessed.

William Congreve

False though she be to me and love,
 I'll ne'er pursue revenge;
For still the charmer I approve,
 Though I deplore her change.

In hours of bliss we oft have met;
 They could not always last:
And though the present I regret,
 I'm grateful for the past.

Sir Walter Ralegh

WALSINGHAM

'As you came from the holy land
 Of Walsingham,
Met you not with my true love
 By the way as you came?'

'How shall I know your true love,
 That have met many one
As I went to the holy land,
 That have come, that have gone?'

'She is neither white nor brown,
 But as the heavens fair,
There is none hath a form so divine
 In the earth or the air.'

'Such an one did I meet, good Sir,
 Such an angelic face,
Who like a queen, like a nymph did appear
 By her gait, by her grace.'

'She hath left me here all alone,
    All alone as unknown,
Who sometimes did me lead with herself,
    And me loved as her own.'

'What's the cause that she leaves you alone
    And a new way doth take,
Who loved you once as her own
    And her joy did you make?'

'I have loved her all my youth,
    But now old as you see,
Love likes not the falling fruit
    From the withered tree.

'Know that Love is a careless child,
    And forgets promise past;
He is blind, he is deaf when he list
    And in faith never fast.

'His desire is a dureless content
    And a trustless joy;
He is won with a world of despair
    And is lost with a toy.

'Of womenkind such indeed is the love
    Or the word love abused,
Under which many childish desires
    And conceits are excused.

'But true Love is a durable fire
    In the mind ever burning;
Never sick, never old, never dead,
    From itself never turning.'

Dante Gabriel Rossetti

AN OLD SONG ENDED

'*How should I your true love know*
  From another one?'
'*By his cockle-hat and staff*
  And his sandal-shoon.'

'And what signs have told you now
  That he hastens home?'
'Lo! the spring is nearly gone,
  He is nearly come.'

'For a token is there nought,
  Say, that he should bring?'
'He will bear a ring I gave
  And another ring.'

'How may I, when he shall ask,
  Tell him who lies there?'
'Nay, but leave my face unveiled
  And unbound my hair.'

'Can you say to me some word
  I shall say to him?'
'Say I'm looking in his eyes
  Though my eyes are dim.'

François Villon

THE OLD LADY'S LAMENT FOR
HER YOUTH

I think I heard the belle
we called the Armouress
lamenting her lost youth;
this was her whore's language:
'Oh treacherous, fierce old age,
you've gnawed me with your tooth,
yet if I end this mess
and die, I go to hell.

'You've stolen the great power
my beauty had on squire,
clerk, monk and general;
once there was no man born
who wouldn't give up all
(whatever his desire)
to have me for an hour –
this body beggars scorn!

'Once I broke the crown's laws,
and fled priests with a curse,
because I kept a boy,
and taught him what I knew –
alas, I only threw
myself away, because
I wanted to enjoy
this pimp, who loved my purse.

'I loved him when he hid
money, or used to bring
home whores and smash my teeth –
Oh when I lay beneath,
I forgave everything –
my tongue stuck to his tongue!
Tell me what good I did?
What's left? Disease and dung.

'He's dead these thirty years,
and I live on, grow old,
and think of that good time,
what was, what I've become;
sometimes, when I behold
my naked flesh, so numb,
dry, poor and small with time,
I cannot stop my tears.

'Where's my large Norman brow,
arched lashes, yellow hair,
the wide-eyed looks I used
to trap the cleverest men?
Where is my clear, soft skin,
neither too brown or fair,
my pointed ears, my bruised
red lips? I want to know.

'Where's the long neck I bent
swanlike, when asking pardon?
My small breasts, and the lips
of my vagina that sat
inside a little garden
and overlooked my hips,
plump, firm and so well set
for love's great tournament?

'Now wrinkled cheeks, and thin
wild lashes; nests of red
string fill the eyes that used
to look and laugh men dead.
How nature has abused
me. Wrinkles plough across
the brow, the lips are skin,
my ears hang down like moss.

'This is how beauty dies:
humped shoulders, barrenness
of mind; I've lost my hips,
vagina, and my lips.
My breasts? They're a retreat!
Short breath – how I repeat
my silly list! My thighs
are blotched like sausages.

'This is how we discuss
ourselves, and nurse desire
here as we gab about
the past, boneless as wool
dolls by a greenwood fire –
soon lit, and soon put out.
Once I was beautiful . . .
That's how it goes with us.'

Translated from the French by
Robert Lowell

W. B. Yeats

CRAZY JANE TALKS WITH THE BISHOP

I met the Bishop on the road
And much said he and I.
'Those breasts are flat and fallen now,
Those veins must soon be dry;
Live in a heavenly mansion,
Not in some foul sty.'

'Fair and foul are near of kin,
And fair needs foul,' I cried.
'My friends are gone, but that's a truth
Nor grave nor bed denied,
Learned in bodily lowliness
And in the heart's pride.

'A woman can be proud and stiff
When on love intent;
But Love has pitched his mansion in
The place of excrement;
For nothing can be sole or whole
That has not been rent.'

Horace

The young bloods come round less often now,
Pelting your shutters and making a row
And robbing your beauty sleep. Now the door
Clings lovingly close to the jamb – though, before,

It use to move on its hinge pretty fast.
Those were the days – and they're almost past –
When lovers stood out all night long crying,
'Lydia, wake up! Save me! I'm dying!'

Soon your time's coming to be turned down
And to feel the scorn of the men about town –
A cheap hag haunting alley places
On moonless nights when the wind from Thrace is

Rising and raging, and so is the fire
In your raddled loins, the brute desire
That drives the mothers of horses mad.
You'll be lonely then and complain how sad

That the gay young boys enjoy the sheen
Of ivy best or the darker green
Of myrtle: dry old leaves they send
As a gift to the east wind, winter's friend.

*Translated from the Latin by
James Michie*

Queen Elizabeth I

When I was fair and young and favour gracèd me,
Of many was I sought, their mistress for to be:
But I did scorn them all, and answered them therefore,
    'Go, go, go, seek some other where:
        Importune me no more.'

How many weeping eyes I made to pine with woe,
How many sighing hearts, I have no skill to show:
Yet I the prouder grew, and answered them therefore,
  'Go, go, go, seek some other where:
        Importune me no more.'

Then spake fair Venus' son, that proud victorious boy,
And said, 'Fine Dame, since that you be so coy,
I will so pluck your plumes that you shall say no more,
  "Go, go, go, seek some other where:
        Importune me no more." '

When he had spake these words, such change grew in my
    breast
That neither night nor day, since that, I could take any
    rest:
Than lo, I did repent that I had said before,
  'Go, go, go, seek some other where:
        Importune me no more.'

Louis Simpson

As birds are fitted to the boughs
That blossom on the tree
And whisper when the south wind blows –
So was my love to me.

And still she blossoms in my mind
And whispers softly, though
The clouds are fitted to the wind,
The wind is to the snow.

Henry Reed

from LESSONS OF THE WAR
JUDGING DISTANCES

Not only how far away, but the way that you say it
Is very important. Perhaps you may never get
The knack of judging a distance, but at least you know
How to report on a landscape: the central sector,
The right of arc and that, which we had last Tuesday,
    And at least you know

That maps are of time, not place, so far as the army
Happens to be concerned – the reason being,
Is one which need not delay us. Again, you know
There are three kinds of tree, three only, the fir and the
       poplar,
And those which have bushy tops to; and lastly
    That things only seem to be things.

A barn is not called a barn, to put it more plainly,
Or a field in the distance, where sheep may be safely
       grazing.
You must never be over-sure. You must say, when
       reporting:
At five o'clock in the central sector is a dozen
Of what appear to be animals; whatever you do,
    Don't call the bleeders *sheep*.

I am sure that's quite clear; and suppose, for the sake of
       example,
The one at the end, asleep, endeavours to tell us
What he sees over there to the west, and how far away,
After first having come to attention. There to the west,
On the fields of summer the sun and the shadows bestow
    Vestments of purple and gold.

The still white dwellings are like a mirage in the heat,
And under the swaying elms a man and a woman
Lie gently together. Which is, perhaps, only to say
That there is a row of houses to the left of arc,
And that under some poplars a pair of what appear to be
      humans
        Appear to be loving.

Well that, for an answer, is what we might rightly call
Moderately satisfactory only, the reason being,
Is that two things have been omitted, and those are
      important.
The human beings, now: in what direction are they,
And how far away, would you say? And do not forget
      There may be dead ground in between.

There may be dead ground in between; and I may not
      have got
The knack of judging a distance; I will only venture
A guess that perhaps between me and the apparent lovers,
(Who, incidentally, appear by now to have finished,)
At seven o'clock from the houses, is roughly a distance
      Of about one year and a half.

Thomas Hardy

UNDER THE WATERFALL

'Whenever I plunge my arm, like this,
In a basin of water, I never miss
The sweet sharp sense of a fugitive day
Fetched back from its thickening shroud of gray.
      Hence the only prime
      And real love-rhyme
      That I know by heart,
      And that leaves no smart,

Is the purl of a little valley fall
About three spans wide and two spans tall
Over a table of solid rock,
And into a scoop of the self-same block;
The purl of a runlet that never ceases
In stir of kingdoms, in wars, in peaces;
With a hollow boiling voice it speaks
And has spoken since hills were turfless peaks.'

'And why gives this the only prime
Idea to you of a real love-rhyme?
And why does plunging your arm in a bowl
Full of spring water, bring throbs to your soul?'

'Well, under the fall, in a crease of the stone,
Though where precisely none ever has known,
Jammed darkly, nothing to show how prized,
And by now with its smoothness opalized,
　　　Is a drinking-glass:
　　　For, down that pass
　　　My lover and I
　　　Walked under a sky
Of blue with a leaf-wove awning of green,
In the burn of August, to paint the scene,
And we placed our basket of fruit and wine
By the runlet's rim, where we sat to dine;
And when we had drunk from the glass together,
Arched by the oak-copse from the weather,
I held the vessel to rinse in the fall,
Where it slipped, and sank, and was past recall,
Though we stooped and plumbed the little abyss
With long bared arms. There the glass still is.
And, as said, if I thrust my arm below
Cold water in basin or bowl, a throe
From the past awakens a sense of that time,
And the glass we used, and the cascade's rhyme.

The basin seems the pool, and its edge
The hard smooth face of the brook side ledge,
And the leafy pattern of china-ware
The hanging plants that were bathing there.
'By night, by day, when it shines or lours,
There lies intact that chalice of ours,
And its presence adds to the rhyme of love
Persistently sung by the fall above.
No lip has touched it since his and mine
In turns therefrom sipped lovers' wine.'

Edwin Morgan

STRAWBERRIES

There were never strawberries
like the ones we had
that sultry afternoon
sitting on the step
of the open french window
facing each other
your knees held in mine
the blue plates in our laps
the strawberries glistening
in the hot sunlight
we dipped them in sugar
looking at each other
not hurrying the feast
for one to come
the empty plates
laid on the stone together
with the two forks crossed
and I bent towards you

sweet in that air
in my arms
abandoned like a child
from your eager mouth
the taste of strawberries
in my memory
lean back again
let me love you
let the sun beat
on our forgetfulness
one hour of all
the heat intense
and summer lightning
on the Kilpatrick hills

let the storm wash the plates

Thomas Hardy

A THUNDERSTORM IN TOWN

(A REMINISCENCE: 1893)

She wore a new 'terra-cotta' dress,
And we stayed, because of the pelting storm,
Within the hansom's dry recess,
Though the horse had stopped; yea, motionless
    We sat on, snug and warm.

Then the downpour ceased, to my sharp sad pain
And the glass that had screened our forms before
Flew up, and out she sprang to her door:
I should have kissed her if the rain
    Had lasted a minute more.

335

Wilfrid Blunt

FAREWELL TO JULIET

I see you, Juliet, still, with your straw hat
Loaded with vines, and with your dear pale face,
On which those thirty years so lightly sat,
And the white outline of your muslin dress.
You wore a little *fichu* trimmed with lace
And crossed in front, as was the fashion then,
Bound at your waist with a broad band or sash,
All white and fresh and virginally plain.
There was a sound of shouting far away
Down in the valley, as they called to us,
And you, with hands clasped seeming still to pray
Patience of fate, stood listening to me thus
With heaving bosom. There a rose lay curled.
It was the reddest rose in all the world.

Stevie Smith

I REMEMBER

It was my bridal night I remember,
An old man of seventy-three
I lay with my young bride in my arms,
A girl with t.b.
It was wartime, and overhead
The Germans were making a particularly heavy raid on
    Hampstead.
Harry, do they ever collide?
I do not think it has ever happened,
Oh my bride, my bride.

Arthur Symons

WHITE HELIOTROPE

The feverish room and that white bed,
The tumbled skirts upon a chair,
The novel flung half-open where
Hat, hair-pins, puffs, and paints, are spread;

The mirror that has sucked your face
Into its secret deep of deeps,
And there mysteriously keeps
Forgotten memories of grace;

And you, half dressed and half awake,
Your slant eyes strangely watching me,
And I, who watch you drowsily,
With eyes that, having slept not, ache;

This (need one dread? nay, dare one hope?)
Will rise, a ghost of memory, if
Ever again my handkerchief
Is scented with White Heliotrope.

W. B. Yeats

CHOSEN

The lot of love is chosen. I learnt that much
Struggling for an image on the track
Of the whirling Zodiac.
Scarce did he my body touch,

Scarce sank he from the west
Or found a subterranean rest
On the maternal midnight of my breast
Before I had marked him on his northern way,
And seemed to stand although in bed I lay.

I struggled with the horror of daybreak,
I chose it for my lot! If questioned on
My utmost pleasure with a man
By some new-married bride, I take
That stillness for a theme
Where his heart my heart did seem
And both adrift on the miraculous stream
Where – wrote a learned astrologer –
The Zodiac is changed into a sphere.

Yehuda Amichai

WE DID IT

We did it in front of the mirror
And in the light. We did it in darkness,
In water, and in the high grass.

We did it in honour of man
And in honour of beast and in honour of God.
But they didn't want to know about us,
They'd already seen our sort.

We did it with imagination and colours,
With confusion of reddish hair and brown
And with difficult gladdening
Exercises. We did it

Like wheels and holy creatures
And with chariot-feats of prophets.
We did it six wings
And six legs

   But the heavens
Were hard above us
Like the earth of the summer beneath.

Translated from the Hebrew by
Harold Schimmel

Louis Simpson

THE CUSTOM OF THE WORLD

O, we loved long and happily, God knows!
The ocean danced, the green leaves tossed, the air
Was filled with petals, and pale Venus rose
When we began to kiss. Kisses brought care,
And closeness caused the taking off of clothes.
O, we loved long and happily, God knows!

'The watchdogs are asleep, the doormen doze . . .'
We huddled in the corners of the stair,
And then we climbed it. What had we to lose?
What would we gain? The best way to compare
And quickest, was by taking off our clothes.
O, we loved long and happily, God knows!

Between us two a silent treason grows,
Our pleasures have been changed into despair.
Wild is the wind, from a cold country blows,
In which these tender blossoms disappear.
And did this come of taking off our clothes?
O, we loved long and happily, God knows!

Mistress, my song is drawing to a close.
Put on your rumpled skirt and comb your hair,
And when we meet again let us suppose
We never loved or ever naked were.
For though this nakedness was good, God knows,
The custom of the world is wearing clothes.

William Soutar

THE TRYSTING PLACE

O luely, luely, cam she in
And luely she lay doun:
I kent her be her caller lips
And her breists sae sma' and roun'.

A' thru the night we spak nae word
Nor sinder'd bane frae bane:
A' thru the nicht I heard her hert
Gang soundin' wi' my ain.

It was about the waukrife hour
When cocks begin to craw
That she smool'd saftly thru the mirk
Afore the day wud daw.

Sae luely, luely, cam she in
Saie luely was she gaen;
And wi' her a' my simmer days
Like they had never been.

luely softly   *bane* bone
caller fresh, cool   *waukrife* waking
sinder'd parted

Paul Dehn

AT THE DARK HOUR

Our love was conceived in silence and must live silently.
This only our sorrow, and this until the end.
Listen, did we not lie all of one evening,
Your heart under my hand

And no word spoken, no, not even the sighing
Of pain made comfortable, not the heart's beat
Nor sound of urgency, but a fire dying
And the cold sheet?

The sailor goes home singing; the lamplit lovers
Make private movements in a public place.
Boys whistle under windows, and are answered;
But we must hold our peace.

Day, too, broke silently. Before the blackbird,
Before the trouble of traffic and the mist unrolled,
I shall remember at the dark hour turning to you
For comfort in the cold.

Sir Edward Dyer

A SILENT LOVE

The lowest trees have tops, the ant her gall,
The fly her spleen, the little spark his heat;
The slender hairs cast shadows, though but small,
And bees have stings, although they be not great;
  Seas have their source, and so have shallow springs;
  And love is love, in beggars and in kings.

Where waters smoothest run, there deepest are the fords,
The dial stirs, yet none perceives it move;
The firmest faith is found in fewest words,
The turtles do not sing, and yet they love;
    True hearts have ears and eyes, no tongues to speak;
    They hear and see, and sigh, and then they break.

W. H. Auden

SONG OF THE MASTER AND BOATSWAIN

At Dirty Dick's and Sloppy Joe's
    We drank our liquor straight,
Some went upstairs with Margery,
    And some, alas, with Kate;
And two by two like cat and mouse
The homeless played at keeping house.

There Wealthy Meg, the Sailor's Friend,
    And Marion, cow-eyed,
Opened their arms to me but I
    Refused to step inside;
I was not looking for a cage
In which to mope in my old age.

The nightingales are sobbing in
    The orchards of our mothers,
And hearts that we broke long ago
    Have long been breaking others;
Tears are round, the sea is deep:
Roll them overboard and sleep.

Thomas Hardy

THE BALLAD-SINGER

Sing, Ballad-singer, raise a hearty tune;
Make me forget that there was ever a one
I walked with in the meek light of the moon
    When the day's work was done.

Rhyme, Ballad-rhymer, start a country song;
Make me forget that she whom I loved well
Swore she would love me dearly, love me long,
    Then – what I cannot tell!

Sing, Ballad-singer, from your little book;
Make me forget those heart-breaks, achings, fears;
Make me forget her name, her sweet sweet look –
    Make me forget her tears.

Edna St Vincent Millay

What lips my lips have kissed, and where, and why,
I have forgotten, and what arms have lain
Under my head till morning; but the rain
Is full of ghosts tonight, that tap and sigh
Upon the glass and listen for reply,
And in my heart there stirs a quiet pain
For unremembered lads that not again
Will turn to me at midnight with a cry.
Thus in the winter stands the lonely tree,
Nor knows what birds have vanished one by one,
Yet knows its boughs more silent than before:
I cannot say what loves have come and gone;
I only know that summer sang in me
A little while, that in me sings no more.

Derek Mahon

GIRLS IN THEIR SEASONS

Girls in their seasons. Solstice and equinox,
This year, make reincarnate
Spry ghosts I had consigned to fate,
Left soaking at the ends of bars,
Pasted in dying calendars
Or locked in clocks.

I can no longer walk the streets at night
But under a lamp-post by a bistro,
To the sound of a zither,
I see one standing in an arc of snow,
Her collar up against the wintry weather
Smoking a cigarette.

Or, as now, slumped by a train window,
The hair of another flies in the air-stream.
This one is here in an advisory
Capacity, reminding me
Of a trip I took last winter
From dream into bad dream.

Their ghosts go with me as I hurtle north
Into the night,
Gathering momentum, age,
Know-how, experience (I travel light) –
Girls, you are welcome to my luggage
For what it is worth.

No earthly schedule can predict
Accurately our several destinations.
All we can do is wash and dress
And keep ourselves intact.
Besides which, this is an express
And passes all the stations.

Now we are running out of light and love,
Having left far behind
By-pass and fly-over.
The moon is no longer there
And matches go out in the wind.
Now all we have

Is the flinty chink of Orion and the Plough
And the incubators of a nearby farm
To light us through to the land of never-never.
Girls all, be with me now
And keep me warm
Before we go plunging into the dark for ever.

John Wilmot, Earl of Rochester

THE DISABLED DEBAUCHEE

As some brave admiral, in former war
   Deprived of force, but pressed with courage still,
Two rival fleets appearing from afar,
   Crawls to the top of an adjacent hill;

From whence, with thoughts full of concern, he views
   The wise and daring conduct of the fight,
Whilst each bold action to his mind renews
   His present glory and his past delight;

From his fierce eyes flashes of fire he throws,
　　As from black clouds when lightning breaks away;
Transported, thinks himself amidst the foes,
　　And absent, yet enjoys the bloody day;

So, when my days of impotence approach,
　　And I'm by pox and wine's unlucky chance
Forced from the pleasing billows of debauch
　　On the dull shore of lazy temperance,

My pains at least some respite shall afford
　　While I behold the battles you maintain
When fleets of glasses sail about the board,
　　From whose broadsides volleys of wit shall rain.

Nor let the sight of honorable scars,
　　Which my too forward valour did procure,
Frighten new-listed soldiers from the wars:
　　Past joys have more than paid what I endure.

Should any youth (worth being drunk) prove nice,
　　And from his fair inviter meanly shrink,
'Twill please the ghost of my departed vice
　　If, at my counsel, he repent and drink.

Or should some cold-complexioned sot forbid,
　　With his dull morals, our bold night-alarms,
I'll fire his blood by telling what I did
　　When I was strong and able to bear arms.

I'll tell of whores attacked, their lords at home;
　　Bawds' quarters beaten up, and fortress won;
Windows demolished, watches overcome;
　　And handsome ills by my contrivance done.

Nor shall our love-fits, Chloris, be forgot,
   When each the well-looked linkboy strove t' enjoy,
And the best kiss was the deciding lot
   Whether the boy fucked you, or I the boy.

With tales like these I will such thoughts inspire
   As to important mischief shall incline:
I'll make him long some ancient church to fire,
   And fear no lewdness he's called to by wine.

Thus, statesmanlike, I'll saucily impose,
   And safe from action, valiantly advise;
Sheltered in impotence, urge you to blows,
   And being good for nothing else, be wise.

Sir Thomas Wyatt

REMEMBRANCE

They flee from me, that sometime did me seek
   With naked foot, stalking in my chamber.
I have seen them gentle, tame, and meek,
   That now are wild, and do not remember
   That sometime they put themselves in danger
     To take bread at my hand; and now they range
     Busily seeking with a continual change.

Thanked be fortune it hath been otherwise
   Twenty times better; but once, in special,
In thin array, after a pleasant guise,
   When her loose gown from her shoulders did fall,
   And she me caught in her arms long and small,
     Therewith all sweetly did me kiss
     And softly said, 'Dear heart, how like you this?'

347

It was no dream; I lay broad waking:
But all is turned, thorough my gentleness,
Into a strange fashion of forsaking;
And I have leave to go of her goodness,
And she also to use newfangleness.
But since that I so kindly am served,
I would fain know what she hath deserved.

Robert Graves

THE WREATH

A bitter year it was. What woman ever
Cared for me so, yet so ill-used me,
Came in so close and drew so far away,
So much promised and performed so little,
So murderously her own love dared betray?
Since I can never be clear out of your debt,
Queen of ingratitude, to my dying day,
You shall be punished with a deathless crown
For your dark head, resist it how you may.

Lord Byron

Remember thee! remember thee!
Till Lethe quench life's burning stream
Remorse and shame shall cling to thee,
And haunt thee like a feverish dream!

Remember thee! Ay, doubt it not.
Thy husband too shall think of thee!
By neither shalt thou be forgot,
Thou *false* to him, thou *fiend* to me!

Arthur Symons

A TUNE

A foolish rhythm turns in my idle head
As a wind-mill turns in the wind on an empty sky.
Why it is when love, which men call deathless, is dead,
That memory, men call fugitive, will not die?
Is love not dead? yet I hear that tune if I lie
Dreaming awake in the night on my lonely bed,
And an old thought turns with the old tune in my head
As a wind-mill turns in the wind on an empty sky.

Ernest Dowson

NON SUM QUALIS ERAM BONAE
SUB REGNO CYNARAE

Last night, ah, yesternight, betwixt her lips and mine
There fell thy shadow, Cynara! thy breath was shed
Upon my soul between the kisses and the wine;
And I was desolate and sick of an old passion,
    Yea, I was desolate and bowed my head:
I have been faithful to thee, Cynara! in my fashion.

All night upon mine heart I felt her warm heart beat,
Night-long within mine arms in love and sleep she lay;
Surely the kisses of her bought red mouth were sweet;
But I was desolate and sick of an old passion,
    When I awoke and found the dawn was gray:
I have been faithful to thee, Cynara! in my fashion.

349

I have forgot much, Cynara! gone with the wind,
Flung roses, roses, riotously with the throng,
Dancing, to put thy pale lost lilies out of mind;
But I was desolate and sick of an old passion,
    Yea, all the time, because the dance was long:
I have been faithful to thee, Cynara! in my fashion.

I cried for madder music and for stronger wine,
But when the feast is finished and the lamps expire,
Then falls thy shadow, Cynara! the night is thine;
And I am desolate and sick of an old passion,
    Yea, hungry for the lips of my desire:
I have been faithful to thee, Cynara! in my fashion.

A. E. Housman

The rainy Pleiads wester,
    Orion plunges prone,
The stroke of midnight ceases
    And I lie down alone.

The rainy Pleiads wester
    And seek beyond the sea
The head that I shall dream of
    That will not dream of me.

Anon

SIXTEENTH CENTURY

Western wind, when will thou blow
    The small rain down can rain?
Christ, if my love were in my arms
    And I in my bed again!

W. B. Yeats

AFTER LONG SILENCE

Speech after long silence; it is right,
All other lovers being estranged or dead,
Unfriendly lamplight hid under its shade,
The curtains drawn upon unfriendly night,
That we descant and yet again descant
Upon the supreme theme of Art and Song:
Bodily decrepitude is wisdom; young
We loved each other and were ignorant.

Donald Davie

TIME PASSING, BELOVED

Time passing, and the memories of love
Coming back to me, carissima, no more mockingly
Than ever before; time passing, unslackening,
Unhastening, steadily; and no more
Bitterly, beloved, the memories of love
Coming into the shore.

How will it end? Time passing, and our passages of love
As ever, beloved, blind
As ever before; time binding, unbinding
About us; and yet to remember
Never less chastening, nor the flame of love
Less like an ember.

What will become of us? Time
Passing, beloved, and we in a sealed
Assurance unassailed
By memory. How can it end,
This siege of a shore that no misgivings have steeled,
No doubts defend?

George Crabbe

A MARRIAGE RING

The ring so worn as you behold,
So thin, so pale, is yet of gold:
The passion such it was to prove;
Worn with life's cares, love yet was love.

John Donne

THE FUNERAL

Whoever comes to shroud me, do not harm
　　　Nor question much
That subtle wreath of hair which crowns mine arm;
The mystery, the sign you must not touch,
　　　For 'tis my outward soul,
Viceroy to that, which then to heaven being gone,
　　　Will leave this to control;
And keep these limbs, her provinces, from dissolution.

For if the sinewy thread my brain lets fall
　　　Through every part,
Can tie those parts, and make me one of all;
These hairs which upward grew, and strength and art

Have from a better brain
Can better do'it; Except she meant that I
By this should know my pain,
As prisoners then are manacled, when they are condemned
to die.

Whate're she meant by it, bury it with me,
For since I am
Love's martyr, it might breed idolatry,
If into others' hands these relics came;
As 'twas humility
To'afford to it all that a soul can do,
So, 'tis some bravery,
That since you would save none of me, I bury some of you.

Robert Lowell

THE OLD FLAME

My old flame, my wife!
Remember our lists of birds?
One morning last summer, I drove
by our house in Maine. It was still
on top of its hill —

Now a red ear of Indian maize
was splashed on the door.
Old Glory with thirteen stripes
hung on a pole. The clapboard
was old-red schoolhouse red.

Inside, a new landlord,
a new wife, a new broom!
Atlantic seaboard antique shop
pewter and plunder
shone in each room.

353

A new frontier!
No running next door
now to phone the sheriff
for his taxi to Bath
and the State Liquor Store!

No one saw your ghostly
imaginary lover
stare through the window,
and tighten
the scarf at his throat.

Health to the new people,
health to their flag, to their old
restored house on the hill!
Everything had been swept bare,
furnished, garnished and aired.

Everything's changed for the best —
how quivering and fierce we were,
there snowbound together,
simmering like wasps
in our tent of books!

Poor ghost, old love, speak
with your old voice
of flaming insight
that kept us awake all night.
In one bed and apart,

we heard the plow
groaning up hill —
a red light, then a blue,
as it tossed off the snow
to the side of the road.

Anonymous Frontier Guard

EIGHTH CENTURY

While the leaves of the bamboo rustle
On a cold and frosty night,
The seven layers of clobber I wear
Are not so warm, not so warm
As the body of my wife.

Translated from the Japanese by
Geoffrey Bownas and Anthony Thwaite

Thomas Hardy

TWO LIPS

I kissed them in fancy as I came
　　Away in the morning glow:
I kissed them through the glass of her picture-frame:
　　She did not know.

I kissed them in love, in troth, in laughter,
　　When she knew all; long so!
That I should kiss them in a shroud thereafter
　　She did not know.

William Wordsworth

She dwelt among the untrodden ways
　　Beside the springs of Dove,
A maid whom there were none to praise
　　And very few to love:

A violet by a mossy stone
    Half hidden from the eye!
—Fair as a star, when only one
    Is shining in the sky.

She lived unknown, and few could know
    When Lucy ceased to be;
But she is in her grave, and, oh,
    The difference to me!

William Barnes

THE WIFE A-LOST

Since I noo mwore do zee your feäce,
    Up steäirs or down below,
I'll zit me in the lwonesome pleäce,
    Where flat-bough'd beech do grow;
Below the beeches' bough, my love,
    Where you did never come,
An' I don't look to meet ye now,
    As I do look at hwome.

Since you noo mwore be at my zide,
    In walks in zummer het,
I'll goo alwone where mist do ride,
    Drough trees a-drippen wet;
Below the raïn-wet bough, my love,
    Where you did never come,
An' I don't grieve to miss ye now,
    As I do grieve at hwome.

Since now bezide my dinner-bwoard
    Your vaïce do never sound,
I'll eat the bit I can avvword,
    A-yield upon the ground;
Below the darksome bough, my love,
    Where you did never dine,
An' I don't grieve to miss ye now,
    As I at hwome do pine.

Since I do miss your vaïce an' feäce
    In praÿer at eventide,
I'll praÿ wi' woone sad vaïce vor greäce
    To goo where you do bide;
Above the tree an' bough, my love,
    Where you be gone avore,
An' be a-waïten vor me now,
    To come vor evermwore.

Emily Brontë

REMEMBRANCE

Cold in the earth, and the deep snow piled above thee!
Far, far removed, cold in the dreary grave!
Have I forgot, my Only Love, to love thee,
Severed at last by Time's all-wearing wave?

Now, when alone, do my thoughts no longer hover
Over the mountains on Angora's shore;
Resting their wings where heath and fern-leaves cover
That noble heart for ever, ever more?

Cold in the earth, and fifteen wild Decembers
From those brown hills have melted into spring –
Faithful indeed is the spirit that remembers
After such years of change and suffering!

Sweet Love of youth, forgive if I forget thee
While the World's tide is bearing me along:
Sterner desires and darker hopes beset me,
Hopes which obscure but cannot do thee wrong.

No other Sun has lightened up my heaven;
No other Star has ever shone for me:
All my life's bliss from thy dear life was given –
All my life's bliss is in the grave with thee.

But when the days of golden dreams had perished
And even Despair was powerless to destroy,
Then did I learn how existence could be cherished,
Strengthened and fed without the aid of joy;

Then did I check the tears of useless passion,
Weaned my young soul from yearning after thine;
Sternly denied its burning wish to hasten
Down to that tomb already more than mine!

And even yet, I dare not let it languish,
Dare not indulge in Memory's rapturous pain;
Once drinking deep of that divinest anguish,
How could I seek the empty world again?

Paul Verlaine

You would have understood me, had you waited;
    I could have loved you, dear! as well as he:
Had we not been impatient, dear! and fated
    Always to disagree.

What is the use of speech? Silence were fitter:
  Lest we should still be wishing things unsaid.
Though all the words we ever spake were bitter,
    Shall I reproach you dead?

Nay, let this earth, your portion, likewise cover
  All the old anger, setting us apart:
Always, in all, in truth was I your lover;
    Always, I held your heart.

I have met other women who were tender,
  As you were cold, dear! with a grace as rare.
Think you, I turned to them, or made surrender,
    I who had found you fair?

Had we been patient, dear! ah, had you waited,
  I had fought death for you, better than he:
But from the very first, dear! we were fated
    Always to disagree.

Late, late, I come to you, now death discloses
  Love that in life was not to be our part:
On your low lying mound between the roses,
    Sadly I cast my heart.

I would not waken you: nay! this is fitter;
  Death and the darkness give you unto me;
Here we who loved so, were so cold and bitter,
    Hardly can disagree.

Translated from the French by
Ernest Dowson

Edgar Allan Poe

TO ONE IN PARADISE

Thou wast that all to me, love,
　For which my soul did pine –
A green isle in the sea, love,
　A fountain and a shrine,
All wreathed with fairy fruits and flowers,
　And all the flowers were mine.

Ah, dream too bright to last!
　Ah, starry Hope! that didst arise
But to be overcast!
　A voice from out the Future cries,
'On! on!' – but o'er the Past
　(Dim gulf!) my spirit hovering lies
Mute, motionless, aghast!

For, alas! alas! with me
　The light of Life is o'er!
No more – no more – no more –
(Such language holds the solemn sea
　To the sands upon the shore)
Shall bloom the thunder-blasted tree,
　Or the stricken eagle soar!

And all my days are trances,
　And all my nightly dreams
Are where thy grey eye glances,
　And where thy footstep gleams –
In what ethereal dances,
　By what eternal streams.

William Wordsworth

Surprised by joy – impatient as the wind
   I turned to share the transport – O! with whom
   But Thee, deep buried in the silent tomb,
That spot which no vicissitude can find?
Love, faithful love, recalled thee to my mind –
   But how could I forget thee? Through what power,
   Even for the least division of an hour,
Have I been so beguiled as to be blind
To my most grievous loss! – That thought's return
   Was the worst pang that sorrow ever bore,
Save one, one only, when I stood forlorn,
   Knowing my heart's best treasure was no more;
That neither present time, nor years unborn
   Could to my sight that heavenly face restore.

William Barnes

SONNET

In every dream thy lovely features rise;
   I see them in the sunshine of the day;
Thy form is flitting still before my eyes
   Where'er at eve I tread my lonely way;
   In every moaning wind I hear thee say
Sweet words of consolation, while thy sighs
Seem borne along on every blast that flies;
   I live, I talk with thee where'er I stray:

And yet thou never more shalt come to me
   On earth, for thou art in a world of bliss,
And fairer still – if fairer thou canst be –

Than when thou bloomed'st for a while in this.
Few be my days of loneliness and pain
Until I meet in love with thee again.

John Clare

TO MARY: IT IS THE EVENING HOUR

It is the evening hour,
   How silent all doth lie,
The hornèd moon he shows his face
   In the river with the sky.
Just by the path on which we pass,
The flaggy lake lies still as glass.

Spirit of her I love,
   Whispering to me,
Stories of sweet visions, as I rove,
   Here stop, and crop with me
Sweet flowers that in the still hour grew,
We'll take them home, nor shake off the bright dew.

Mary, or sweet spirit of thee,
   As the bright sun shines tomorrow.
Thy dark eyes these flowers shall see,
   Gathered by me in sorrow.
In the still hour when my mind was free
To walk alone – yet wish I walked with thee.

Alfred Lord Tennyson

IN THE VALLEY OF CAUTERETZ

All along the valley, stream that flashest white,
Deepening thy voice with the deepening of the night,
All along the valley, where thy waters flow,
I walked with one I loved two and thirty years ago.
All along the valley, while I walked today,
The two and thirty years were a mist that rolls away;
For all along the valley, down thy rocky bed,
Thy living voice to me was as the voice of the dead,
And all along the valley, by rock and cave and tree,
The voice of the dead was a living voice to me.

Thomas Hardy

THE VOICE

Woman much missed, how you call to me, call to me,
Saying that now you are not as you were
When you had changed from the one who was all to me,
But as at first, when our day was fair.

Can it be you that I hear? Let me view you, then,
Standing as when I drew near to the town
Where you would wait for me: yes, as I knew you then,
Even to the original air-blue gown!

Or is it only the breeze, in its listlessness
Travelling across the wet mead to me here,
You being ever dissolved to wan wistlessness,
Heard no more again far or near?

Thus I; faltering forward,
Leaves around me falling,
Wind oozing thin through the thorn from norward,
And the woman calling.

Alfred Lord Tennyson

Oh! that 'twere possible,
After long grief and pain,
To find the arms of my true-love
Round me once again!

When I was wont to meet her
In the silent woody places
Of the land that gave me birth,
We stood tranced in long embraces,
Mixed with kisses sweeter, sweeter,
Than any thing on earth.

A shadow flits before me –
Not thou, but like to thee.
Ah God! that it were possible
For one short hour to see
The souls we loved, that they might tell us
What and where they be.

It leads me forth at evening,
It lightly winds and steals
In a cold white robe before me,
When all my spirit reels
At the shouts, the leagues of lights,
And the roaring of the wheels.

Half the night I waste in sighs,
    In a wakeful doze I sorrow
For the hand, the lips, the eyes –
    For the meeting of tomorrow,
        The delight of happy laughter,
The delight of low replies.

Walter Savage Landor

ROSE AYLMER

Ah, what avails the sceptred race!
    Ah, what the form divine!
What every virtue, every grace!
    Rose Aylmer, all were thine.

Rose Aylmer, whom these wakeful eyes
    May weep, but never see,
A night of memories and sighs
    I consecrate to thee.

Christina Rossetti

ECHO

Come to me in the silence of the night;
    Come in the speaking silence of a dream;
Come with soft rounded cheeks and eyes as bright
    As sunlight on a stream;
        Come back in tears,
O memory, hope, love of finished years.

O dream how sweet, too sweet, too bitter sweet,
  Whose wakening should have been in Paradise,
Where souls brimfull of love abide and meet;
  Where thirsting longing eyes
    Watch the slow door
That opening, letting in, lets out no more.

Yet come to me in dreams, that I may live
  My very life again though cold in death:
Come back to me in dreams, that I may give
  Pulse for pulse, breath for breath:
    Speak low, lean low,
As long ago, my love, how long ago.

Pablo Neruda

Tonight I can write the saddest lines.

Write, for example, 'The night is shattered
and the blue stars shiver in the distance.'

The night wind revolves in the sky and sings.

Tonight I can write the saddest lines.
I loved her, and sometimes she loved me too.

Through nights like this one I held her in my arms.
I kissed her again and again under the endless sky.

She loved me, sometimes I loved her too.
How could one not have loved her great still eyes.

Tonight I can write the saddest lines.
To think that I do not have her. To feel that I have lost
   her.

To hear the immense night, still more immense without
   her.
And the verse falls to the soul like dew to the pasture.

What does it matter that my love could not keep her.
The night is shattered and she is not with me.

This is all. In the distance someone is singing. In the
   distance.
My soul is not satisfied that it has lost her.

My sight searches for her as though to go to her.
My heart looks for her, and she is not with me.

The same night whitening the same trees.
We, of that time, are no longer the same.

I no longer love her, that's certain, but how I loved her.
My voice tried to find the wind to touch her hearing.

Another's. She will be another's. Like my kisses before.
Her voice. Her bright body. Her infinite eyes.

I no longer love her, that's certain, but maybe I love her.
Love is so short, forgetting is so long.

Because through nights like this one I held her in my arms
my soul is not satisfied that it has lost her.

Though this be the last pain that she makes me suffer
and these the last verses that I write for her.

Translated from the Spanish by
W. S. Merwin

C. P. Cavafy

TO REMAIN

It must have been one or one-thirty
after midnight.
        In a corner of the wine-shop;
behind the wooden partition.
Except for the two of us, the shop was completely deserted.
An oil lamp scarcely burning.
The waiter who had been awake,
slept now at the door.

No one would see us. But
we were so excited anyway
we couldn't take precautions.

We partly undid our clothes – there weren't many
as it was in divine burning July.

Enjoyment of flesh through
half-torn clothes;

368

quickly bared flesh; apparition
twenty-six years passed; and now returned
to remain in this poetry.

Translated from the Greek by
Nikos Stangos and Stephen Spender

Dylan Thomas

IN MY CRAFT OR SULLEN ART

In my craft or sullen art
Exercised in the still night
When only the moon rages
And the lovers lie abed
With all their griefs in their arms,
I labour by singing light
Not for ambition or bread
Or the strut and trade of charms
On the ivory stages
But for the common wages
Of their most secret heart.

Not for the proud man apart
From the raging moon I write
On these spindrift pages
Nor for the towering dead
With their nightingales and psalms
But for the lovers, their arms
Round the griefs of the ages,
Who pay no praise or wages
Nor heed my craft or art.

Thomas Hardy

IN TIME OF 'THE BREAKING OF NATIONS'

Only a man harrowing clods
    In a slow silent walk
With an old horse that stumbles and nods
    Half asleep as they stalk.

Only thin smoke without flame
    From the heaps of couch-grass;
Yet this will go onward the same
    Though Dynasties pass.

Yonder a maid and her wight
    Come whispering by:
War's annals will cloud into night
    Ere their story die.

Acknowledgements

The editor gratefully acknowledges permission to reproduce copyright poems in this book.

FLEUR ADCOCK: From *Tigers* by Fleur Adcock. Copyright © Oxford University Press, 1967. Reprinted by permission of the publisher.

ANNA AKHMATOVA: 'I wrung my hands' from *Poems of Akhmatova*, translated by Max Hayward and Stanley Kunitz, by permission of Atlantic-Little, Brown & Co. Copyright © 1973 by Max Hayward and Stanley Kunitz.

YEHUDA AMICHAI: 'We Did It' from *Songs of Jerusalem and Myself* by Yehuda Amichai, translated by Harold Schimmel (Harper & Row, 1973), 'Quick and Bitter' and 'A Pity. We Were Such a Good Invention' from *Poems* by Yehuda Amichai, translated by Assia Gutmann. Copyright © 1968 by Yehuda Amichai. English translation copyright © 1968, 1969 by Assia Gutmann. All included in *Selected Poems* by Yehuda Amichai, Penguin Books, 1971. Reprinted by permission of Harper & Row, Publishers, Inc., Olwyn Hughes and Penguin Books.

ANON: 'Plucking the Rushes', from *170 Chinese Poems*, translated by Arthur Waley, Constable & Co. Ltd; and from *Translations from the Chinese* by Arthur Waley. Copyright 1919, 1941 by Alfred A. Knopf, Inc., renewed 1947 by Arthur Waley. Reprinted by permission of the publishers.

ANON: 'The Wife's Complaint', from *The Earliest English Poems*, translated by Michael Alexander, Penguin Books, 1966.

ANONYMOUS FRONTIER GUARD: From *The Penguin Book of Japanese Verse*, translated by Geoffrey Bownas and Anthony Thwaite, Penguin Books, 1964.

GUILLAUME APOLLINAIRE: Translated by Quentin Stevenson. From *The Succession*, Oxford University Press. By permission of the translator.

W. H. AUDEN: 'Dear, though the night is gone', copyright 1935 by W. H. Auden, 'Fish in the unruffled lakes', copyright 1937, renewed 1965 by W. H. Auden, and 'Lay your sleeping head, my love', copyright 1940, renewed 1968 by W. H. Auden, all from *Collected Shorter Poems 1927–1957* by W. H. Auden; 'Master and

371

Boatswain' from 'The Sea and the Mirror', copyright 1944 by W. H. Auden, from *Collected Longer Poems* by W. H. Auden. Reprinted by permission of Faber & Faber Ltd and Random House, Inc.

CHARLES BAUDELAIRE: Translated by Roy Campbell. Reprinted by permission of Hughes Massie Ltd.

HILAIRE BELLOC: From *Complete Verse*, Gerald Duckworth & Co. Ltd. Reprinted by permission of A. D. Peters & Company.

JOHN BERRYMAN: No. 36 and No. 71 from *Berryman's Sonnets*, No. 4 from *77 Dream Songs* and No. 171 from *His Toy, His Dream, His Rest*, to Faber & Faber Ltd; reprinted with the permission of Farrar, Straus & Giroux, Inc. from *The Dream Songs* by John Berryman. Copyright © 1959, 1962, 1963, 1964, 1965, 1966, 1967, 1968, 1969 by John Berryman.

JOHN BETJEMAN: From *Collected Poems*. Reprinted by permission of the author and John Murray (Publishers) Ltd.

BHARTRHARI: From *Poems from the Sanskrit*, translated by John Brough, Penguin Books, 1968.

LUIS DE CAMOËNS: Translated by Roy Campbell. From *Collected Poems Vol. III* by Roy Campbell, reprinted by permission of The Bodley Head Ltd.

ROY CAMPBELL: 'The Sisters' from *Adamastor*, Faber & Faber, reprinted by permission of Curtis Brown Ltd.

CATULLUS: No. 45 and No. 92 from *The Poems of Catullus*, translated by Peter Whigham, Penguin Books, 1966.

C. P. CAVAFY: 'To Remain' from *Fourteen Poems*, translated by Nikos Stangos and Stephen Spender, Editions Alecto, London, 1968. Reprinted by permission of the translators; 'On the Street' from *The Complete Poems of C. P. Cavafy*, translated by Rae Dalven. Reprinted by permission of The Hogarth Press and Harcourt Brace Jovanovich, Inc.

ALAIN CHARTIER: From *Towards Silence* by Edward Lucie-Smith. Copyright © Oxford University Press, 1968. Reprinted by permission of the publisher.

AUSTIN CLARKE: From *Collected Poems*. Reprinted by permission of The Dolmen Press, Dublin.

TONY CONNOR: From *With Love Somehow* by Tony Connor. Copyright © Oxford University Press, 1962. Reprinted by permission of the publisher.

JOHN CORNFORD: By permission of Mr Christopher Cornford.

HART CRANE: From *The Collected Poems and Selected Letters and Prose of Hart Crane* by Hart Crane. Reprinted by permission of

ACKNOWLEDGEMENTS

Oxford University Press and Liveright Publishing, New York. Copyright © 1933, 1958, 1966 by Liveright Publishing Corp.

ROBERT CREELEY: 'The Way' by Robert Creeley from *For Love*. Copyright © 1962 by Robert Creeley. Reprinted by permission of Calder & Boyars Ltd and Charles Scribner's Sons.

E. E. CUMMINGS: 'it may not always be so; and i say . . .', copyright 1923, 1951 by E. E. Cummings, 'if i should sleep with a lady called death' and 'i like my body when it is with your body', copyright 1925 by E. E. Cummings, 'somewhere i have never travelled', copyright 1931, 1959 by E. E. Cummings, 'may i feel said he', copyright 1935 by E. E. Cummings. All reprinted from his volume *Complete Poems 1913–1962* by permission of MacGibbon & Kee and Harcourt Brace Jovanovich, Inc.

DONALD DAVIE: From *A Winter Talent and Other Poems*, 1957. Reprinted by permission of Routledge & Kegan Paul Ltd.

C. DAY LEWIS: From *Collected Poems*, 1954. Copyright 1954 by C. Day Lewis. Reprinted by permission of the Executors of the Estate of C. Day Lewis, Jonathan Cape Ltd, The Hogarth Press and Harold Matson Co., Inc.

PAUL DEHN: From *The Fern on the Rock*. Copyright © 1965 by Paul Dehn. Reprinted by permission of Hamish Hamilton, London.

LAWRENCE DURRELL: From *Collected Poems* by Lawrence Durrell. Copyright © 1956, 1960 by Lawrence Durrell. Reprinted by permission of Faber & Faber Ltd and E. P. Dutton & Co., Inc.

T. S. ELIOT: From *Collected Poems 1909–1962*. Reprinted by permission of Faber & Faber Ltd and Harcourt Brace Jovanovich, Inc.

PAUL ÉLUARD: Translated by Quentin Stevenson. From *The Succession*, Oxford University Press. By permission of the translator.

HARRY FAINLIGHT: From *Sussicran*, published by Turret Books. Reprinted by permission of the author.

LAWRENCE FERLINGHETTI: 'Away Above a Harborful' from *A Coney Island of the Mind*. Copyright 1955 by Lawrence Ferlinghetti. Reprinted by permission of New Directions Publishing Corporation, New York.

ROBERT GRAVES: From *Collected Poems* by Robert Graves, Cassell & Co. Ltd, 1965. Reprinted by permission of the author.

THOM GUNN: From *Fighting Terms*. Reprinted by permission of Faber & Faber Ltd.

HAFIZ: From *Thirty Poems*, translated by Peter Avery and John Heath-Stubbs. Reprinted by permission of John Murray (Publishers) Ltd.

ACKNOWLEDGEMENTS

THOMAS HARDY: From *Collected Poems*. Copyright 1925 by The Macmillan Company, renewed 1953 by Lloyds Bank Ltd. Reprinted by permission of the Trustees of the Hardy Estate, Macmillan, London and Basingstoke, The Macmillan Company of Canada Limited and Macmillan Publishing Co., Inc., New York.

JOHN HEATH-STUBBS: From *Selected Poems*, Oxford University Press. Reprinted by permission of the author.

ANTHONY HECHT: 'Going the Rounds' first printed in the *Quarterly Review of Literature*, 1969. Reprinted by permission of the author.

HEDYLOS: By permission of the translator, Louis Untermeyer. Copyright 1956 by Louis Untermeyer.

LADY HEGURI: From *The Penguin Book of Japanese Verse*, translated by Geoffrey Bownas and Anthony Thwaite, Penguin Books, 1964.

A. D. HOPE: From *Collected Poems 1930–1965* by A. D. Hope. Copyright 1963, 1966 in all countries of the International Copyright Union by A. D. Hope. All rights reserved. Reprinted by permission of The Viking Press, Inc. and Angus & Robertson (U.K.) Ltd.

HORACE: From *Poems of Horace*, Rupert Hart-Davis. Reprinted by permission of the translator, James Michie.

A. E. HOUSMAN: 'When I was one-and-twenty' and 'Oh, when I was in love with you' from 'A Shropshire Lad' – Authorized Edition – from *The Collected Poems of A. E. Housman*. Copyright 1939, 1940, © 1965 by Holt, Rinehart and Winston, Inc. Copyright © 1967, 1968 by Robert E. Symons; 'The rainy Pleiads wester' from *The Collected Poems of A. E. Housman*. Copyright 1936 by Barclays Bank Ltd. Copyright © 1964 by Robert E. Symons. Reprinted by permission of The Society of Authors as the literary representative of the Estate of A. E. Housman, Jonathan Cape Ltd, and Holt, Rinehart & Winston, Inc., Publishers, New York.

TED HUGHES: 'September' from *The Hawk in the Rain* by Ted Hughes. Copyright © 1957 by Ted Hughes. Reprinted by permission of Faber & Faber Ltd and Harper & Row, Publishers, Inc.

ELIZABETH JENNINGS: From *Collected Poems*. Reprinted by permission of Macmillan, London and Basingstoke.

ST JOHN OF THE CROSS: Translated by Roy Campbell. Reprinted by permission of Hughes Massie Ltd.

DONALD JUSTICE: Reprinted from *The Summer Anniversaries* by Donald Justice by permission of Wesleyan University Press. Copyright © 1954 by Donald Justice.

PHILIP LARKIN: From *The Whitsun Weddings*. Reprinted by permission of Faber & Faber Ltd.

D. H. LAWRENCE: From *The Complete Poems of D. H. Lawrence*,

edited by Vivian de Sola Pinto and F. Warren Roberts. Copyright ©
1964, 1971 by Angelo Ravagli and C. M. Weekley, Executors of
the Estate of Frieda Lawrence Ravagli. All rights reserved. Reprinted
by permission of The Viking Press, Inc., Lawrence Pollinger Ltd and
the Estate of the late Mrs Frieda Lawrence.

LAURIE LEE: From *The Sun My Monument*. Reprinted by permission
of the author and The Hogarth Press.

ALUN LEWIS: 'Goodbye' from *Ha, Ha, Among the Trumpets* and
'Postscript: For Gweno' from *Raider's Dawn*. Reprinted by permis-
sion of George Allen & Unwin Ltd.

FEDERICO GARCIA LORCA: From *Lament for the Death of a Bull-
fighter and Other Poems*, translated by A. L. Lloyd. Copyright ©
1962 by A. L. Lloyd. Reprinted by permission of New Directions
Publishing Corporation, New York, publishers and agents for the
Estate of Federico Garcia Lorca.

ROBERT LOWELL: 'Man and Wife' from *Life Studies*, copyright ©
1958 by Robert Lowell; 'The Old Flame' from *For the Union Dead*,
copyright © 1962 by Robert Lowell; and Villon, 'The Old Lady's
Lament for Her Youth' from *Imitations*, copyright © 1958, 1959,
1960, 1961 by Robert Lowell. Reprinted by permission of Faber
& Faber Ltd and Farrar, Straus & Giroux, Inc.

HUGH MACDIARMID: From *Collected Poems* by Hugh MacDiarmid.
Copyright © Christopher Murray Grieve, 1948, 1962. Reprinted by
permission of Macmillan Publishing Co., Inc.

ARCHIBALD MACLEISH: From *The Collected Poems of Archibald
MacLeish*. Reprinted by permission of Houghton Mifflin Company.

LOUIS MACNEICE: From *Collected Poems of Louis MacNeice*, edited
by E. R. Dodds. Copyright © The Estate of Louis MacNeice, 1966.
Reprinted by permission of Faber & Faber Ltd and Oxford University
Press, Inc.

DEREK MAHON: From *Night Crossing* by Derek Mahon. Copyright ©
Oxford University Press, 1968. Reprinted by permission of the pub-
lisher.

MARTIAL: From *After Martial* by Peter Porter. Copyright © Oxford
University Press, 1972. Reprinted by permission of the publisher.

MATURAI ERUTTĀḼAṈ CĒNTAMPŪTAṈ: From *The Interior
Landscape*, translated by A. K. Ramanujan, published by Peter Owen,
London, and Indiana University Press, Reprinted by permission of the
publishers.

MELEAGER: 'Love's night and a lamp' and 'Busy with love, the
bumble bee' from *The Poems of Meleager*, 1973. Reprinted by per-
mission of the translator, Peter Whigham, and Anvil Press Poetry.

ACKNOWLEDGEMENTS

CHARLOTTE MEW: From *Collected Poems*, 1953. Reprinted by permission of Gerald Duckworth & Co. Ltd.

HAROLD MONRO: From *Collected Poems*, 1970. Reprinted by permission of Gerald Duckworth & Co. Ltd.

EDWIN MORGAN: By permission of the author.

EDWIN MUIR: From *Collected Poems 1921–1958* by Edwin Muir. Copyright © 1960 by Willa Muir. Reprinted by permission of Faber & Faber Ltd and Oxford University Press Inc.

VLADIMIR NABOKOV: Reprinted by permission of the author. Copyright © 1944, 1972 by Vladimir Nabokov. All rights reserved.

PABLO NERUDA: 'Tonight I can write the saddest lines' from *Twenty Love Poems and a Song of Despair* by Pablo Neruda, translated by W. S. Merwin. Translation copyright © 1969 by W. S. Merwin. Reprinted by permission of Jonathan Cape Ltd and Grossman Publishers; 'Drunk as drunk on turpentine' from *The Man Who Told His Love*, translated by Christopher Logue. Reprinted by permission of Scorpion Press.

BORIS PASTERNAK: Reprinted by permission of the translators, Peter France and Jon Stallworthy.

BRIAN PATTEN: From *Little Johnny's Confession*. Copyright © Brian Patten, 1967. Reprinted by permission of George Allen & Unwin Ltd and Farrar, Straus & Giroux, Inc.

OCTAVIO PAZ: From *Configurations*. Copyright © 1968 by Octavio Paz and Charles Tomlinson. Reprinted by permission of Jonathan Cape Ltd and New Directions Publishing Corporation.

PETRONIUS: 'Good God, what a night that was', from *Poems from the Greek Anthology*, translated by Kenneth Rexroth. Reprinted by permission of The University of Michigan Press.

EZRA POUND: From *Collected Shorter Poems*, Faber & Faber, and *Personae*, New Directions Publishing Corporation. Copyright 1926 by Ezra Pound. Reprinted by permission of the publishers.

JOHN PRESS: From *Guy Fawkes Night*, Oxford University Press. Reprinted by permission of the author.

JACQUES PRÉVERT: 'Alicante', translated by Lawrence Ferlinghetti, copyright © 1947 by Les Editions du Point du Jour. Reprinted by permission of City Lights Books.

JONATHAN PRICE: By permission of the author.

F. T. PRINCE: By permission of the author.

ALEXANDER PUSHKIN: Translated by Reginald Mainwaring Hewitt. Reprinted by permission of Basil Blackwell.

JOHN CROWE RANSOM: From *Selected Poems*, *Third Edition*,

Revised and Enlarged, by John Crowe Ransom. Copyright 1927 by Alfred A. Knopf, Inc. and renewed 1955 by John Crowe Ransom. Reprinted by permission of Eyre & Spottiswoode (Publishers) Ltd and Alfred A. Knopf, Inc.

W. R. RODGERS: From *Europa and the Bull.* Reprinted by permission of Martin Secker & Warburg Ltd.

THEODORE ROETHKE: 'She', copyright © 1956, and 'I Knew a Woman', copyright 1954 by Theodore Roethke, from the book *Collected Poems of Theodore Roethke.* Reprinted by permission of Faber & Faber Ltd and Doubleday & Company, Inc.

PIERRE DE RONSARD: By permission of the translator, Robert Mezey.

ALAN ROSS: From *African Negatives.* Reprinted by permission of Eyre & Spottiswoode (Publishers) Ltd.

RUDAKI: From *Loquitor.* Translated by Basil Bunting. Reprinted by permission of Fulcrum Press.

LOUIS SIMPSON: 'As birds are fitted to the boughs' (copyright © 1955 by Louis Simpson), which first appeared in *Discovery 6*, is reprinted by permission of Oxford University Press from *Selected Poems* by Louis Simpson, and Charles Scribner's Sons from *Poets of Today II* by Louis Simpson *et al.*; 'The Custom of the World', copyright © 1949 by Louis Simpson. Reprinted from *A Dream of Governors* by Louis Simpson, by permission of Wesleyan University Press.

STEVIE SMITH: From *Selected Poems,* Copyright © 1962, 1964 by Stevie Smith. Reprinted by permission of Longman and New Directions Publishing Corporation.

W. D. SNODGRASS: From *After Experience* by W. D. Snodgrass, published by Oxford University Press and Harper & Row, Publishers, Inc. Copyright © 1966 by W. D. Snodgrass. Reprinted by permission of the publishers.

WILLIAM SOUTAR: Reprinted by permission of The Trustees of the National Library of Scotland.

STEPHEN SPENDER: From *Collected Poems 1928–1953*, Faber & Faber Ltd; and from *Selected Poems*, by Stephen Spender, Random House, Inc. Copyright 1942 by Stephen Spender. Reprinted by permission of the publishers.

ARTHUR SYMONS: From *Collected Poems.* Reprinted by permission of Martin Secker & Warburg Ltd.

DYLAN THOMAS: From *Collected Poems.* Reprinted by permission of J. M. Dent & Sons and the Trustees for the copyrights of the late Dylan Thomas; and from *The Poems of Dylan Thomas.* Copyright 1946

ACKNOWLEDGEMENTS

by New Directions Publishing Corporation. Reprinted by permission of New Directions Publishing Corporation, New York.

R. S. THOMAS: From *Song at the Year's Turning*. Reprinted by permission of Hart-Davis Ltd.

FRANÇOIS VILLON: Translated by Robert Lowell. From *Imitations*, copyright © 1958, 1959, 1960, 1961 by Robert Lowell. Reprinted by permission of Faber & Faber Ltd and Farrar, Straus & Giroux, Inc.

ANDREI VOZNESENSKY: 'Dead Still' translated by Richard Wilbur and included in *Antiworlds* by Andrei Voznesensky, edited by Patricia Blake and Max Hayward, published by Oxford University Press and Basic Books Inc. Copyright © by Basic Books Inc., Publishers, New York. Reprinted by permission of the publishers.

RICHARD WEBER: From *Stephen's Green Revisited*. Reprinted by permission of The Dolmen Press, Dublin.

HUGO WILLIAMS: From *Symptoms of Loss*, by Hugo Williams. Copyright © Oxford University Press, 1965. Reprinted by permission of the publishers.

W. B. YEATS: From *Collected Poems*. 'When You Are Old' and 'Never Give All the Heart' copyright 1906 by The Macmillan Company, renewed 1934 by William Butler Yeats; 'A Drinking Song' and 'Brown Penny' copyright 1912 by The Macmillan Company, renewed 1940 by Bertha Georgie Yeats; 'Crazy Jane Talks with the Bishop', 'Chosen', 'Lullaby', 'A Last Confession' and 'After Long Silence' copyright 1933 by The Macmillan Company, renewed 1961 by Bertha Georgie Yeats; 'Whence Had They Come' copyright 1934 by The Macmillan Company, renewed 1962 by Bertha Georgie Yeats. Reprinted by permission of Mr M. B. Yeats, The Macmillan Company of London and Basingstoke, The Macmillan Company of Canada Ltd and Macmillan Publishing Co., Inc.

Every effort has been made to trace copyright holders, but in a few cases this has proved impossible. The publishers would be interested to hear from any copyright holders not here acknowledged.

Index of Poets and Translators

Index of Titles and First Lines

Note: titles are given in *italics*. † after an entry indicates that the text has been modernized.